A case for the Enlightenment, ten essays

Frits Van Holthoon

A case for the Enlightenment, ten essays

These essays were published separately in the *European Journal*, Vincenzo Merolle ed. .
The essays were published in Dutch:
F.L. van Holthoon, *Terug naar de Verlichting*, (Budel 2013: Damon).

Bibliographic information published by the Deutsche Nationalbibliothek

The Deutsche Nationalbibliothek lists this publication in the Deutsche Nationalbibliografie; detailed bibliographic data are available on the Internet at http://dnb.d-nb.de .

Cover image: Anicet-Charles-Gabriel Lemonnier: Reading of Voltaire's "L'Orphelin de la Chine" in the Salon of Madame Geoffrin, (Malmaison, 1812).

ISBN 978-3-8325-4447-8

Logos Verlag Berlin GmbH
Comeniushof, Gubener Str. 47,
10243 Berlin
Germany
phone: +49 (0)30 42 85 10 90
fax: +49 (0)30 42 85 10 92
http://www.logos-verlag.de

A case for the Enlightenment, ten essays

Preface

Why would someone want to write about the Enlightenment again? My mundane reason was that I had to write a syllabus for a set of lectures meant for an audience of the Senior Academy in Groningen. Writing it I discovered that there are still a lot of clichés attached to the Enlightenment, which obscure the true nature of this eighteenth-century phenomenon. The clichés are my reason to try to set the record straight. Critics pro and contra the Enlightenment base their arguments mostly on a nineteenth-century interpretation of it. My ambition in the essays which follow is to return to the eighteenth-century scene and try to interpret the bearers of the Enlightenment in their own words and ideas. Obviously this has been done before and serious scholars usually are not the victims of the clichés, but the clichés are very persistent and need to be combated persistently. This becomes particularly true in our time, when critics of the Enlightenment accuse it of being responsible for the global crisis we are experiencing, while they mistake its true nature. Perhaps I can offer a very modest contribution to the debate on its true nature and make us ask what we still can learn from the Enlightenment.

Many sympathetic readers have helped me to clear my thoughts. Two friends should be mentioned in particular. Roger Emerson of the University of Western Ontario and Bruce Kuklick of the University of Pennsylvania have corrected my English and peppered my texts with their remarks. Often when I sent them a text I got it back the next day. I wish to thank them both in the warmest terms; they have helped me enormously in accomplishing my task. Recently Vincent Hope went through the text again and corrected some typos and irregularities. I am also grateful to him.

F.L. van H.

1. What is the Enlightenment?

Nature, Nature's Laws lay hid in Night.
God said, *let Newton be*, and *All* was *Light*
(Alexander Pope)

1. Introduction

The Enlightenment: we accept the label without reflection. It suggests a closely knit organization of philosophers and *literati* who preached a consistent doctrine. And the amazing thing is that there is such a unity, perhaps not of doctrine but rather of purpose. The Enlightenment is not so much a movement but a network of writers who knew other writers personally or knew about them. Granted we should speak of Enlightenments rather than the Enlightenment. In the German speaking countries, in France, in Italy and Great Britain the accents were different, but there is enough unity of effort and purpose in the writings of certain eighteenth-century authors to allow us to speak of *the* Enlightenment.

There are scholars, who argue that there was no Enlightenment in England, but surely Pope's *Essay on Man* is an Enlightenment tract. The Scottish Enlightenment is an accepted notion and so it should be for England as Roy Porter has made clear in his *Enlightenment, Britain and the Creation of the Modern World.*[1] Voltaire was the first to notice the English Enlightenment in his *Lettres Philosophiques*[2] and the message of his English exile was that the Enlightenment really *started* in England. Pope glorified Newton, because the man with his theory of gravity pro-

[1] See *Bibliographical Notice.*

[2] Voltaire wrote his *Lettres* in England where he was banished after a quarrel with the chevalier de Rohan. Rohan ordered his valets to give Voltaire a beating. When Voltaire brought a lawsuit against Rohan he was put in the Bastille with the choice to leave for England or stay there.

vided the capstone in the new cosmological theory which we call the scientific revolution and Pope himself introduced a new chapter to it: the study of man. That study became the major preoccupation of the Enlightenment philosophers.

There are many clichés connected with the accepted image of the Enlightenment. One of them is that the writers of the Enlightenment were first of all rationalists. As always with clichés this interpretation of the Enlightenment message is not totally wrong, but it misses the point. In his *Treatise of Human Nature* Hume gave two definitions of reason.[3] Reason is first of all the instinct of logical deduction. That gift is a useful tool, but – in his famous saying – "Reason is and *ought* only to be the slave of the passions."[4] That is the proper definition of reason, because the passions motivate us to act and without an understanding of our passions reason cannot help us to use them in a useful way. Secondly we have the capacity to be reasonable and that involves an improper definition of reason, because being reasonable is the effect of a passion and has nothing to do with our logical instinct and everything with our sentiments. The Enlightenment is often presented as The Age of Reason. In my opinion The Age of Sentiment is a better label. *Sentiment* became an exciting term in the eighteenth century. Our feelings move us to act and so it is essential that we explore them and learn what causes them. Sentiments provide the motives, which make us act and learning about them brings us to the threshold of morality and moral judgments. How can we not see how important sentiment was to the writers of the Enlightenment when we read Rousseau's *La Nouvelle Héloïse*? The exploration of sentiment became such a major preoccupation that Laurence Sterne wrote a satire – so at least I think – on it in his *Sentimental Journey*.

In what follows I shall develop four maxims:

---

[3] Reason as logical faculty Hume defines as a "wonderful and unintelligible instinct in our souls" [*Treatise of Human Nature* (Oxford 1978: Clarendon Press), P.H. Nidditch ed., I, 3, xvi, 179; elsewhere [THN, II, 3, iii, 417] he writes that the calm passion of reasonableness "is confounded with reason by all those, who judge of things from the first view and appearance."

[4] THN, II, 3, iii, 415; notice the *ought*.

1. We can argue when the Enlightenment started, but not when it ended.
2. Though the objectives of the Enlightenment are the same everywhere in Europe there is a great divide between Britain and the continent which is caused by the economic development of Britain.
3. A sense of balance manifested itself in art, economics and politics, because writers aspired to a harmony of sentiments as the outcome of this balance.
4. The writers of the Enlightenment accepted the regimes under which they lived. They wanted to reform the *société des ordres,* not to abolish it. When these reforms would be a success this would mean the end of history.

A treatment of these maxims will provide my answer to the question: what is the Enlightenment?

2. The End of the Enlightenment

When did it start? Hazard concluded that Locke's *Essay* and his two *Treatises* started the systematic inquiry into the possibilities of a secular morality and a new form of politics.[5] This is an attractive view. Rejecting innate ideas Locke provided the formula for morality on a secular basis and by participating in ecumenical protestant movement he infused that secular morality with Christian values. That was what the Enlightenment needed. Locke's *Essay Concerning Human Understanding* and his *Reasonableness of Christianity* had a funneling effect, because ideas since 1680 converged in his work and provided a platform for the Enlightenment. Recently this view was challenged by Jonathan Israel who has made Spinoza the messenger of a more radical Enlightenment with emphasis on personal freedom and democracy. There are two problems with this interpretation. How radical were Spinoza's ideas and how great was his influence on eighteenth-century writers? My answer to the first question is that Spinoza's ideas on democracy and freedom of expression were less radical than they appear to Israel. As to Spinoza's influence, the paradoxical conclusion is that his influence should have been substantial, but it was not, at

[5] P. Hazard, *La Crise de la Conscience Européenne 1680-1715* (Paris 1961: Fayard).

John Locke

least in France. Paul Verrière has shown that French writers, with few exceptions, did not read Spinoza, but all knew Bayle's lemma in his *Dictionnaire.*[6] It was Bayle who settled Spinoza's reputation of being an atheist and a pantheist. Hume who probably never read Spinoza, confirmed to this conventional and wrong interpretation of Spinoza's philosophy.[7] It was only in Germany that the *Aufklärer* recognized the true message of Spinoza's *Ethics* that passion leads to reason and reason leads to God.

Scholars such as Margaret Jacob and Robert Darnton who have studied the shady characters of Grub Street and their counterparts on the continent have added an interesting chapter to eighteenth-century studies, but it is not a chapter that belongs to the history of the Enlightenment.[8] For that was a movement of the establishment and as I shall

[6] P. Vernière, *Spinoza et la Pensée Française avant la Révolution* (Paris 1954: PUF) dl.2, 526 en 608.

[7] F.L. van Holthoon, "Spinoza and Hume, Two Different Trajectories", *2000. The European Journal,* 2011, XII(1).

[8] M.C. Jacob, *The Radical Enlightenment. Pantheists, Freemasons and Republicans,* (London 1981: Allen & Unwin); R. Darnton, *The Literary Underground of*

argue in a next section it is wrong to regard it as a radical movement that prepared the road to the French Revolution.

When did the Enlightenment end? The French Revolution abolished not only the monarchy, but also the culture of the salons and the *Encyclopédie*. In France the years between 1750 and 1770 were the culmination of the Enlightenment when France was regarded as the centre of civilization. In the seventies the mood changed in France and elsewhere. In the expectation of the convocation of the *États Généraux* conversations became more political and new people joined in. In Germany and Britain it was the revolution itself that constituted the clean break with the past. Condorcet epitomized the nature of the break. During the fifties he was a man of the establishment. He embraced the revolution (as the only member of the Enlightenment) and his *Esquisse* introduced the idea of progress stating that mankind would progress to perfection. The idea that mankind *will* progress turned the idea of progress into a theory.[9]

3. Enlightenment, Enlightenments: Britain and the Continent

Two key-concepts of the Enlightenment are modernization and secularization.

a. *Modernization* in a contemporary context means a process of change driven by technological innovation, as applied to the eighteenth-century it concerns the well functioning of society, and the priority of this program of eighteenth century modernization was the development of agriculture. In this respect Britain was in advance of most European countries. The enclosures of medieval open field villages and the emergence of free tenants culminated in an agriculture in which landlords on their often vast estates cooperated with farmers who acted as manufacturers by investing capital in their agricultural

---

the Old Regime (Cambridge Mass. 1982: Harvard UP). Many of the French revolutionaries were respectable men with respectable careers before the revolutionaries, but they had no entry to the salons of the establishment and resented this fact.

[9] Condorcet, *Esquisse d'un Tableau Historique des Progrès de l'Esprit Humain* (1795).

production.[10] The landlords invested in the infrastructure of their estates and their tenants (the capitalist farmers) invested in equipment and new farming techniques. The so-called agricultural revolution was the basis of the growth of industrial activities and commercial expansion. Economists such as David Hume and Adam Smith preached economic liberty and were severe critics of monopolies. Economic actors should be left to pursue their own interests, but both authors added the important proviso that the state should interfere in the economic process, when its authority was in danger of being subverted. The ability of the Hanoverian regime to maintain order was as much part of the success of modernization in eighteenth-century Britain as economic expansion itself.

On the continent modernization was seen as a task of the central government. Freeing the peasants from feudal burdens was the first priority. The *Physiocrats* in France looked with admiration at the British scene. They wanted to promote the existence of *fermiers* at the expense of the overburdened and unproductive peasants. With the reforms they proposed they had two objectives in mind, 1. Raising the agricultural productivity and 2. Reforming the tax system. The latter objective was of crucial importance, for the existing system was oppressive and worse, ineffectual. In a brief moment of glory Turgot as minister of finance seemed to be able to realize their reforms. His dismissal showed that the royal government was totally incapable of pursuing any policies.

Observers have often wondered why the French Revolution could so easily blow away the cobwebs of feudalism, but it may have been so that both tenants and landowners came to regard the seigneurial dues as oppressive, because the modernization of the rural economy was already taking place, surreptitiously, and largely unobserved.

Reformers therefore supported the central governments in their efforts to free the peasants. Hence the popularity of "enlightened des-

---

[10] See D. Ricardo, *The Principles of Political Economy and Taxation* (London 1965: Everyman's Library). Ricardo considered it the normal of business that farmers would invest capital, see ch. VI "On Profits".

Pierre Bayle

pots" such as the Austrian emperors Joseph II and Leopold II, Frederick of Prussia and Catherine of Russia. Their policies were high-handed and timid at the same time and did not free the peasants. In Austria and Prussia the only significant, material product of the Enlightenment, was a new and much needed civil and penal code.

In surveying the efforts at economic reform we should realize that the political and social *status quo* was never put in question. Reforms should take place within what was called the "society of orders". That statement applies as well to Britain as countries on the continent.

Modernization had older roots than secularization. Max Weber traced the start of the process to the beginning of Western civilization. His thesis that Calvinism promoted the emergence of capitalism - the so-called 'Weber-thesis' – is an important chapter in this process. The discussion on how and if Calvinism promoted capitalism is endless. Trevor Roper made a sensible remark in this respect:

> In other words we must look on the explanation of our problem [the Weber-thesis], not so much in Protestantism and the expelled entrepreneurs as in Catholicism and the expelling societies.[11]

Indeed modernizing tendencies were fought tooth and nail while in protestant countries the authorities favoured or at least tolerated them. What made the case of the Enlightenment special was that secularization became the main impulse of modernization.

b. *Secularization* meant finding the alternative to the prescription of Christian orthodoxy in regard to morality, politics, economics, and history. The secularization of morality came first. All the writers of the Enlightenment insisted that moral rules should be made on earth and were not to be decided in heaven. Hume phrased their claim as follows:

> It is only experience, which teaches us the nature and bounds of cause and effect, and enables us to infer the existence of one object from that of another. Such is the foundation of moral reasoning, which forms the greater part of human knowledge, and is the source of all human action and behaviour.[12]

This claim earned writers the reputation of being atheists, but their situation was much more complicated than this reputation suggests. Obviously Hume's saying was deeply offensive to divines in Great Britain, because it undermined the authority of their priesthood. However, there were many protestant clergymen – the latitudinarians in England and the moderates in Scotland – who tacitly accepted it and though squabbles between them would suggest otherwise, they and their counterparts in other protestant countries were the foot soldiers of the Enlightenment.

In France all *philosophes* were anticlericals and with good reason. The sometimes cruel and always ridiculous behaviour of the Catholic

---

[11] 12 H.R. Trevor Roper, *Religion, the Reformation and Social Change*, (London 1977: Macmillan), 19.

[12] D. Hume, *An Enquiry Concerning Human Understanding* (Oxford 2000: Clarendon Press), T. L. Beauchamp ed., 122.

D'Alembert

Church merited their hostility, but the *philosophes* were not necessarily atheists. Voltaire wrote that he was not a Christian but that he loved God as his friend.[13] Voltaire could be called a deist and in this respect he had many followers in France.

The *Encyclopédie* which started to be published in 1751 is the best example how all-encompassing the effort at the secularization of knowledge was. D'Alembert in his *Discours Préliminaire* divided knowledge in three compartments: *Mémoire, Raison* and *Imagination.* The second column of knowledge contained all the useful and scientific subjects. Biblical history, *l'histoire sacrée*, was in the first column and to add to its insult of neglect its place in the first column indicated that it was a thing of the past. Recently Pocock has added a new chapter to the study of the Enlightenment. In volume two of his series on *Barbarism and Religion*, he shows how Voltaire in his *Essai sur les*

[13] P. Pomeau, *La Religion de Voltaire*, (Paris 1969: Nizet).

Moeurs created an alternative to biblical history which found its last and eloquent instalment in Bossuet's *Histoire Universelle.*[14] Voltaire eliminated providence as the key-concept of Bossuet's history and replaced it by the concept of *moeurs.* Including a discussion of Chinese and Indian civilization in universal history, he wanted to show how civilized manners reached its perfected form in his own time.

The contrast between Britain and the continent (particularly France) meant that Britain enacted modernization and on the continent philosophers talked about it. As to secularization the conclusion must be that there is no divide between Britain and the continent. The age of the Enlightenment was not an anti-religious period, but compared to the century that followed many philosophers did not take religion very seriously and the theologians who did, could not stop the secularization of morality, even in their own ranks. Secularization, eighteenth-century style, scored the victory that the case for Revelation became a question of faith, not of evidence. Though many nineteenth-century writers took religion much more seriously than their eighteenth-century counterparts, they could not escape this conclusion.

4. A Harmony of Sentiments

If I had to sum up the Enlightenment in one word it would be *balance.* Balance is a key word in Du Bos and Reynolds' aesthetic theories, balance is at the centre of Montesquieu and Hume's political theories; balance is the input of eighteenth-century moralists who aspired to a balance of sentiments.

Sentiment to the eighteenth-century observer is that psychical phenomenon which is provoked by our confrontation with the outside world. Sentiments are the material of our moral judgments and turn into passions when they have been processed in our soul. That processing is the reason why Hume defined passions as 'impressions of reflection'.[15] I quote Hume, because I know his work best, but the at-

[14] J. G. A. Pocock, *Barbarism and Religion,* vol. 2, *Narratives of Civil Government* (Cambridge 1999: Cambridge University Press).

[15] D. Hume, THN, II, 1, I, 275.

tention to sentiment was widespread among eighteenth-century writers. Passions had always been an important subject in metaphysics, but in the eighteenth-century reaching the goal of a balance of sentiments became a major preoccupation of moralists.

The goal was important for aesthetic and pragmatic reasons. Individuals aspired to this balance of sentiments and so they should, because as Hume argued this balance was the only way in which they could cooperate amicably and create a moral economy that would maximize their pleasures.

One of the red herrings of the study of Adam Smith is the so-called 'Adam Smith problem'. The German scholar Skarzynski maintained that there is an inconsistency in Smith's thought when we compare the altruistic tone of Smith's *Theory of Moral Sentiments* and the egoistic motivation which Smith took for granted in his *Wealth of Nations.*[16] However, there is no inconsistency. Smith said, in both works, that if people were left to their own devices they would cooperate for their mutual benefit. The promotion of happiness, being the outcome of this cooperation, was an idea fundamental to the program of the Enlightenment. Helvétius wrote in the preface of his *De l'Esprit*

> ...qu'en lisants ces Discours, on s'apercevra que j'aime les hommes, que je désire leur bonheur, sans haïr ni mépriser aucun d'eux en particulier.[17]

Helvétius saw the clergy as the enemy of well-being, but he was not an atheist. That is rather surprising, because his formula for happiness is self-sufficient – not needing God's intervention or command – but there was a metaphysical residue which lifted the experience of happiness to a higher plane. The aesthetic lift was the second goal of striving for a balance of sentiments leading to a harmony of sentiments. The sense of happiness is first of all the consciousness that

---

[16] W. von Skarzynski, *Adam Smith als Moralphilosoph und Schöpfer der Nationaloekonomie,* (Berlin 1878), discussed in D.D. Raphael & A.L Macfie, "Introduction", Adam Smith, *The Theory of MoralSentiments,* (Oxford 1976: Clarendon Press), 20ff.

[17] Helvétius, *De l'Esprit* (Paris 1959: Editions Sociales), G. Besse ed., 69.

one's soul is in harmony.[18] For many writers of the Enlightenment there was the urge to attribute this feeling of harmony to a higher power, not to let this power interfere in their lives, but accept it as a metaphysical expression of this feeling of happiness.

5. The End of History

Francis Fukuyama created quite a stir when he introduced the concept of The End of History. It meant that the future would hold no surprises as long as mankind would stick to certain simple (liberal) rules on how to cooperate. Later Fukuyama had to confess that he had underestimated the impact of the Industrial Revolution which is still causing a compound of unintended effects which makes the world highly unstable and volatile and is disrupting the liberal paradise.

I use the term Enlightenment to indicate that the philosophers accepted the society of orders in which they lived as the final stage of civilization. It could be reformed, but it was impossible to change its structure. That is a surprising conclusion, because within that structure there literally was no place for many individuals, vagrants, beggars, but also workmen in Paris or London who lived there not being under control of the police and not being registered. And the treatment of the common man, who had a place in the society of orders, was often brutal and unjust. Hume called the press gang – the sordid method of recruiting men for the British fleet – peculiar. That is hardly the comment of a man much concerned with social justice. Voltaire's campaign for the rehabilitation of that unfortunate draper Jean Calas who was tortured to death protesting his innocence shocked everyone in France and abroad, but Voltaire never put in question the system of justice.[19] Beccaria was successful in his plea for the abolishment of

[18] The search for happiness is "La recherche des équilibres" between the forces of nature, society and reason, R. Mauzi writes in *L'Idée du Bonheur dans la Littérature et la Pensée Française au XVIIIIIème Siècle* (Paris 1960: Colin), 64.

[19] In his *Lettre sur la Tolérance* (1763) Voltaire described the judicial murder of Calas, but a large part dealt with the persecution of the Huguenots and Voltaire's focus was on intolerance not on justice. Calas was a Huguenot and the rumour went that his son wanted to convert to Catholicism and that his father

Condorcet

torture as a technique of interrogating suspects. He was less successful with his idea of scrapping the death penalty. The reaction to his *Dei Delitti e Delle Pene* was part of that humanitarian impulse that was older and more universal than the movement of the Enlightenment, but except when focused on an unfortunate victim remained rather vague and unspecific.

In a future essay I shall argue that a theory of progress was virtually absent in the eighteenth century. The philosophers believed in reforming persons, not in changing structures and institutions. The idea that human history will *inevitably* lead to progress in the future,

wanted to prevent this by murdering his son. The rumour was untrue and Calas was manifestly innocent.

was absent. That idea was launched in Condorcet's *Esquisse*, but that work is a product of the French Revolution.

This is a controversial statement; do let me explain what I mean by it. David Spadafora has written a substantial book on *The Idea of Progress in Eighteenth-Century Britain*[20] and certainly there was an *idea* of progress, also elsewhere in Europe. It meant that people had the feeling that their lives were much more civilized than those of their ancestors. As to the explanation on how they got there *theories* were not so clear and decisive. The four stages theory (explored by Ronald Meek[21]) is an example of such a theory not well worked out. Decisive is that there was no expectation and hence no *theory* (until Condorcet) that mankind *must* progress, because that is mankind's destiny.

Historians who have studied the Industrial Revolutions may find it easy, with the wisdom of hindsight, to ask how eighteenth-century philosophers could be so blind as not to notice the first signs of it and the vast potentiality of reform that it would offer. However they saw their world evolving out of age old structures which brought their restraints with them. The economic cycle which Quesnay introduced in his *Tableau Économique* was not primarily a recipe for economic growth, but was in the first place a demonstration for the better functioning of the rural economy. Its main concern was not the profitability of agriculture, but to create the conditions for tax reform. There was a sense of urgency in their plans for reform. The Physiocrats and their ally Turgot were fully aware that the Ancien Régime would collapse if the much needed reforms would not be implemented. As indeed it did introducing the French Revolution.

It was not only that the eighteenth-century philosophers did not see what could replace the society of orders; they also did not want to see it replaced. The maintenance of authority was an important goal in itself. Hume shared this belief in authority with the Physiocrats:

---

[20] (New Haven 1990: Yale University Press).

[21] R. Meek, *Social Science and the Ignoble Savage* (Cambridge 1976: Cambridge University Press).

> In this sense [a system that admits of a participation of power within the rule of law], it must be owned, that liberty is the perfection of civil society; but still authority must be acknowledged essential to its very existence: and in those contests, which so often take place between the one and the other, the latter may, on that account, challenge the preference.[22]

Order is in the nature of things according to Shakespeare:

> The heavens themselves, the planets, and this centre,
> Observe degree, priority and place
> Insisture, course, proportion, season, form,
> Office, and custom, in all line of order.[23]

All creatures have their fixed place in the Great Chain of Being; Man has it within society. Of course the Physiocrats and the British economists were aware that some things within society will change, but that the Industrial Revolution would change society out of recognition was something they could not see. Take Adam Smith's *Wealth of Nations*. He advocated not growth but a stable economy (of which growth could be a pleasant by-product). Take his definition of the classical factors of production. Labour fixed a man's position in the social order, and became a commodity of exchange. Resources meant in the first place agricultural produce that determined the well-being of society and was responsible for the power relations within society. Agriculture became just one sector in an industrial economy and the landed society lost its political clout. Capital was defined by Adam Smith as hoarded labour, i.e. you must have it before you can invest it. Afterwards capital got the function of a credit facility and you did not necessarily have to save in order to invest. You could speculate on future yields. Sometimes someone set a door ajar, looked into a future where everything was in flux and quickly closed a door on a nightmare which could not possibly come true. Order was more than a method to keep the rabble at bay. It was a way of life.

---

[22] D. Hume, "Of the Origin of Government", *Essays, Moral, Political and Literary* (Indianapolis 1987: Liberty*Classics*), E.F. Miller ed., 41.

[23] W. Shakespeare, "Troilus and Cressida", *The Complete Works* (London 1923: Collins), 758.

The Enlightenment was, as I see it, a movement within the established classes. Talleyrand remarked that those who had not witnessed the coming and goings of the Ancien Régime did not know how sweet life could be. That may have been true for the upper classes, but not for the common man. If only for that reason we cannot retrace our steps. However a harmony of sentiments could be an important legacy to us amidst the predicament of credit crises. On the long run we are not in the position to want more, but we can always aspire to better things. That is how I see the message of the Enlightenment to us, if we decide to look for it.

2. The Networking of the Enlightenment

1. Melchior Grimm's *Correspondance Littéraire*

In terms of human relations the Enlightenment was a case of networking with a peculiar character. Networking meant that people met each other in clubs, reading academies and societies and of course the famous Parisian *salons.* They published their writings not only in books or pamphlets (and broadsides), but also in letters. Letters often circulated to more people than the addressee. Many were written with an eye on publication or they were passed around among friends.

Melchior Grimm was the prototype of a net-worker. He came to Paris as a young graduate of the University of Regensburg and soon moved in cliques associated with the Enlightenment. Grimm started his *Correspondance Littéraire* in 1753 and kept it going until 1774 when he turned his business over to Jakob Heinrich Meister. Every fortnight he sent handwritten letters to German courts, the Swedish court and the Archduke of Tuscany. In his letters he told his correspondents everything which took place in the fashionable world of France.

Grimm's business (for it was a business; he was paid by subscription though the princely readers did not pay him very well or regularly) is remarkable for several reasons.

In the first place he wrote to his correspondents to bring them news on French culture and the scandals of upper class society, emphasizing the fact that Paris was the spider in the web of the Enlightenment in France. Secondly, he wrote to his royals without becoming their stooge. He dealt with them on equal terms. He had the news they wanted. Evidently the royals took a lively interest in the *faits divers* of the Enlightenment and they did not regard all these writings as being subversive of their exalted positions. Rather their enthusiasm in itself was subversive for it meant that they no longer believed in the orthodox doctrines of state or church, even though they had to uphold them for obvious reasons. From his side Grimm was not alone among the philosophers and *literati* of the Enlightenment in regarding the ruling princes as instruments of reform. Reform in his estimation had to be applied top down.

Thirdly, the *Correspondance Littéraire* did not discuss political affairs. The focus of the more serious news was on art, literature and the philosophy of human nature and by and large these topics formed the focus of the Enlightenment. When Grimm stopped writing his *CL* he became something of a diplomat and a go-between between princes and writers. Since he met Catherine of Russia he did errands for her, buying books, jewels and paintings and during the years 1789 and 1790 when the French Revolution came into full swing, he became her informant on events in Paris. That ended when he was forced to leave the city and his property was being sequestered by the revolutionary government. Grimm from then on lived on Catherine's subsidies.

Fourthly, the *Correspondance Littéraire* is remarkably indiscrete, at least by our standards. So Grimm reports a love poem that Voltaire sent to his mistress Mme de Châtelet, and though Voltaire repeatedly warned his correspondents to be careful with showing his letters to others, Grimm's *CL* is proof that many found a much wider circulation. Voltaire used this fact to conceal his own indiscretions washing his hands in innocence. Emile Lizé has registered 886 pieces which relate to Voltaire in the *CL.*[1] That is a remarkable number, because relations between the 'patriarch' (Voltaire) and the 'prophète' (Grimm) were far from friendly, but Voltaire was always news and Grimm admired the man. Voltaire personified the independent role of the intellectual who dealt with the high and mighty on his own terms. And when at the court of Frederick of Prussia they were not met he left though under painful circumstances. It was a role which the *philosophes* claimed for themselves. This claim I think explains the reports on love affairs and scandals in Grimm's *CL.* The high and mighty and the *philosophes* were *entre nous* in the business of the Enlightenment.

---

[1] E. Lizé, *Voltaire, Grimm et la Correspondance Littéraire* (Oxford 1979: The Voltaire Foundation: Studies on Voltaire and the Eighteenth Century, 180).

Melchior Grimm

The 'patriarch' Voltaire was the unofficial leader of the *philosophes.* That is a problematic statement, because Voltaire had a strict neo-classical conception of the relations of state, church and society which few of the *philosophes* shared. He thoroughly disapproved of Rousseau's style of thinking and writing; he frowned upon the blunt atheism of the Baron d'Holbach. There were different groups of *philosophes* who met in the *salons.* You had the circle of atheists who gathered in the salon of d'Holbach (vividly described by Philipp Blom in his study *Wicked Company*).[2] There was the group around Diderot who wrote for the *Encyclopédie,* and then there were the *économistes* who met in an entresol of the palace of Versailles where *maître* Quesnay led the discussion on agrarian reform.

Voltaire was at the periphery of all these groups, if only for the reason that he had to live at the periphery of France for most of his adult life. Yet from Cirey (the estate of Mme de Châtelet and her husband),

[2] Ph. Blom, *Wicked Company,Freethinkers and Friendship in Pre-Revolutionary Paris* (London 2011; Weidenfeld & Nicolson).

and later at Ferney near Geneva, he sent out his letters and manuscripts. It is estimated he wrote 120.000 letters. Besterman's modern edition contains 21.200 letters of which 15.000 are by Voltaire. From his outpost he influenced everybody and the authorities were powerless to act against his flood of advice, satire and serious criticism. Voltaire had one asset which protected him. He was a firm supporter of the establishment, but he demanded that the leaders of church and state should become more enlightened (I will deal with his ideas on this when discussing his *Siècle de Louis XIV* in a subsequent essay).

After a beating by the thugs of the Chevalier de Rohan, Voltaire started a lawsuit against Rohan and was sent to the Bastille. There he was given the choice to leave France or stay in prison. Voltaire never forgot the haughtiness of the nobleman and swore that he would never accept it in the future. Voltaire went to London. The intellectual freedom he experienced in England was a tonic to him. In due time, he produced his report on England in his *Lettres Philosophiques* (1734).[3] Its Parisian edition was immediately banned by the authorities. There were many offensive passages in the *Lettres*, such as: where there is one church you have despotism, two churches mean civil war, "mais il y en a trente, et elles vivent en paix et heureuses."[4] However Voltaire's general message must have shocked the authorities. England was presented as a successful state with a thriving civil society because of the existence of intellectual freedom. After the *Lettres Philosophiques* he became the frontrunner of the Enlightenment.

To the French public Voltaire was first of all known as a writer of plays. Some of them are produced occasionally, but I think it is fair to say that they are no longer appreciated very much. Voltaire was a strong believer in the neo-classical model for writing poems and plays. He considered his panegyric on Henri IV, the *Henriade*, his greatest

---

[3] An English version appeared in 1733.

[4] Voltaire, *Lettres Philosophiques* (Paris 1986: Gallimard), 61. This dictum reminds one of Madison's saying in *Federalist LI* : "In a free government, the security for civil rights must be the same as for religious rights. It consists in the one case in the multiplicity of interests, and in the other, in the multiplicity of sects." (ed. Cooke, Meridian books), 351-352.

achievement. For the historian this epic poem is fascinating because of its implicit criticism of the government of Louis XV, but for the general reader it must be dreary stuff, as is the case with all his poems and plays.

We remember Voltaire for his *Candide* and his campaign for religious tolerance and fair justice. It was Voltaire who successfully lobbied for the rehabilitation of Jean Calas. It was the way he presented this case of judicial murder which mesmerized the public and forced the authorities to accept the verdict of the public: never again. The unfortunate draper from Toulouse was slowly tortured to death protesting his innocence of the death of his son who hanged himself in his father's workshop. It was said that the father, who was a Huguenot, had murdered his son in order to prevent his conversion to Catholicism. It was typically a case of persecution and judicial stupidity. In his *Traité sur la Tolérance* Voltaire broadened the issue by pleading for the religious freedom of the still remaining Huguenots in France

As a critic Voltaire presents an interesting case. He pursued the authorities with satire, witticism (he had an irresistible impulse to deliver them) and serious criticism. His net-working made him a formidable opponent.

2. The Encyclopédie

What we need, Fontenelle wrote, is new knowledge. We should give up our immoderate admiration for ancient knowledge and promote the expertise we need to develop a new sense of sociability.[5] New knowledge! The *Encyclopédie ou Dictionnaire Raisonné des Sciences, des Arts et des Métiers* fulfilled Fontenelle's dearest wish. D'Alembert wrote the preface for the undertaking[6] and Diderot accepted the main burden of editing the folios of text, 17 in total en 11 volumes of engravings. The first volume appeared in 1751 and after the last volume was published in 1772 he gave up the editorship. A few years later

[5] R. Marchal, *Fontenelle à l'Aube des Lumières* (Paris 1997: Champion), 158.

[6] He wrote a number of articles on mathematics and a lemma on Geneva which caused a scandal, because he observed that most of the Genevan pastors had Socinian leanings.

the publisher Panckouke bought the rights. Robert Darnton has described the intricate history of the reprints in full detail.[7] In the course of years 24.900 sets were sold, the part of the first edition was 4225 sets.

Gradually Panckouke's undertaking became a mixture of old and new knowledge. The old tended to become obsolete after the French Revolution. Take all the entries on feudal laws and privileges. The revolution had abolished all feudal privileges with one stroke, so these entries only had historical interest. The new contributions had a different character. Diderot and his contributors wanted to educate public opinion, the contributions in Panckouke's undertaking wanted to inform. However, the greatest difference between Diderot and Panckouke's business was that the latter had no trouble with the authorities. Diderot constantly ran the risk that his work would be sequestered and that he would land in jail. In fact both events happened, but Diderot had the protection of the director of censorship (!) and could continue his work. So the contributors and their editor had to be careful in what they wrote. However, Diderot could not resist making little jokes (he shared this habit with Voltaire). So the heathen ritual *Ypainy* hinted at the Eucharist as a parallel example. Diderot introduced cross-references written in the margin of entries of contributors. So a cross-reference in the entry *Cordeliers* referred to the entry *Capuchon* making it clear that the monks of this order were perpetually quarrelling about the size of their monks cap. Apart from these impish jokes there were many instances of serious criticism. Diderot himself wrote "Le mot *intolérance* s'entend communément de cette passion féroce qui porte à haïr et à persécuter ceux qui sont dans l'erreur." Intolerance is a bad example of violence towards those who think and believe differently.[8] The Chevalier de Jaucourt, a Protestant from Geneva, wrote a well-informed critique of the French tax system and famous are the two lemmata that Quesnay contributed on *Grain* and *Fermiers* in which he expounded the physiocratic plans for agrar-

7 R. Darnton, *The Business of Enlightenment. A Publishing History of the* Encyclopédie, *1775-1800* (Cambridge Mass. 1979: Harvard University Press).

8 J. Lough, *The Encyclopédie* (Genève 1989: Slatkine reprints), 198-199.

ian reform. But though the tone of contributions to the *Encyclopédie* was measured and respectful the enemies of the *Encyclopédie* were not taken in. Omer Joli de Fleuri, Advocate General of the Parliament of Paris, wrote:

> A l'ombre d'un dictionnaire qui rassemble une infinité de notions utiles et curieuses sur les arts et les sciences on y fait entrer une compilation alphabétique de toutes les absurdités, de toutes les impiétés répandues dans tous les auteurs; on les a embellies, augmentées, mises dans un jour plus frappant. Ce dictionnaire est composé dans le goût de celui de Bayle. On y développe, selon les articles, le *pour* et le *contre*; mais le *contre*, quand il s'agit de la religion, y est toujours exposé clairement et avec affectation.[9]

And you have only to read d'Alembert's famous *Discours Préliminaire* to discover what was at stake. The *Encyclopédie* presented a programme of secular knowledge or sacred knowledge which was presented from a secular point of view. In his Baconian diagrammatical scheme d'Alembert divided all knowledge into three columns reflecting *la mémoire, la raison* and *l'imagination.* In the first column history figured including *l'histoire sacrée.* The third column was devoted to the arts and the second column contained all useful knowledge derived from natural science and the philosophy of human nature. The second column was evidently the most important and with its emphasis on useful knowledge and its anti-metaphysical bias it made the *Encyclopédie* the major compendium of the ideas of the French Enlightenment.[10]

The clerical critics were well aware of the danger of the propaganda for factual knowledge the *Encyclopédie* was making. The reading

---

[9] Quoted by J. Lough, *The Encyclopédie* (Genève 1989: Slatkine reprints), 123.

[10] The clerics protested against the neglect of l'histoire sacrée. The historian Edward Gibbon as a young man protested against the neglect of erudite knowledge. His *essai* was a first sample of the historicist attitude which nineteenth-century historians would adopt. See J.G.A. Pocock, *Barbarism and Religion,* vol. 1, *The Enlightenments of Edward Gibbon, 1737-1764* (Cambridge 1999: Cambridge University Press), 137 ff.

public in France and elsewhere was small. About 50% of the French population was illiterate and of the literature only a small proportion of them were accomplished readers. This was a bourgeois audience of noblemen, merchants, craftsmen, some enterprising farmers and professionals. Traditionally the Church had wielded its hegemonic power over these classes of people. Now the Church had a formidable rival to cope with and gradually the priests lost their audience to the *Encyclopédistes.* The latter were no revolutionaries in the strict sense. Yet their impact on the *Ancien Régime* was revolutionary. And we can illustrate this impact by Hume's last sentence in his *Enquiry Concerning Human Understanding*:

> If we take in our hand any volume; of divinity or school metaphysics, for instance; let us ask, *Does it contain any abstract reasoning concerning quantity or number?* No. *Does it contain any experimental reasoning concerning matter of fact and existence?* No. Commit it then to the flames: For it can contain nothing but sophistry and illusion.[11]

3. The Salons

In their heyday, between 1750 and 1770, the topics of the *Encyclopédie* were discussed in the Parisian *salons.* Perhaps the most spectacular fact of the existence is that they made it clear that the court at Versailles was no longer the centre of French culture as under Louis XIV. If you were accepted as a guest you might like David Hume make a tour of different *salons* during the week. *If* you were accepted: for admittance you needed wit, talent and connections. The Girondin Brissot de Warville carried a grudge against the *salons,* because he never was admitted.

In Italy at the Renaissance courts groups of men developed the manners for a polite conversation about arts and sciences. The ideal of politesse reached the court of the French King François I and served as a counterweight to the rough and violent behaviour of the French

[11] D. Hume, *An Enquiry Concerning Human Understanding* (Oxford 2000: Clarendon Press), 123.

nobility. Catherine of Rambouillet (the name of the 'hotel' she had built in Paris to receive her guests) established a *salon* with the express purpose of promoting a civilised conversation and her *salon* became the prototype of the eighteenth-century ones.

In the eighteenth century, clubs and societies sprung up everywhere in Europe. They were the product of an expanding economy in which the bourgeoisie took the lead. In England clubs were organized in coffee houses and the interesting aspect of their emergence is that they quickly spread to overseas parts of the expanding British Empire. All these clubs in Britain had the function to put the relations between the bourgeoisie and the nobility on an easy basis. That function was also the express purpose of freemason lodges.

The intermingling of bourgeois intellectuals and noblemen also occurred in the French *salons*, but otherwise the *salons* presented a different type of gathering. British clubs, including the lodges, were exclusively for men[12] and the clubs did not foster an ideal of civilised behaviour. Members quarrelled, gambled and drank to excess; the lodges obviously being an exception. The only politesse which was accepted was the politesse of the duel. The ideal of politesse was promoted elsewhere in Britain, for instance in the *Spectator* of Addison and Steele.

The French *salons* were run by women mostly (the *salons* of d'Holbach and Helvétius were exceptions). In the first half of the eighteenth century noble women exploited the *salon*, but in the heyday bourgeois women took over. Mme Geoffrin, who held her *salons* between 1749 and 1776, was one these hostesses. Born as Marie Thérèse Rodet she was married as a young girl to the director of the glass-works of Saint Gobain. She was semi-literate. Her grandmother, who educated her, judged that a girl only needs to know how to read, not to write. After a life as a dutiful wife, Mme Geoffrin started her *salon* over the protests of her husband (who now is only remembered as her husband). She had a thirst for knowledge and her *salon* was her education. Being a true *bourgeoise* she firmly kept order in her *salon*,

[12] Later lodges for women came into existence.

no drunkenness, no bawdy jokes, no gambling. The *salon* was her way to enter high-society that is the world of the nobility. However, the interesting aspect of her *salon* – in fact of all *salons* – is that she put her bourgeois stamp on the social relations where nobility and bourgeois intellectuals met. Another hostess, Mme Necker (wife of the banker Necker who played an important role in the prologue to the French Revolution) jotted down in her notebook: be careful to keep the attention of your guests, prepare for it, because the success of the conversation in your *salon* depends on it.[13]

The position these women acquired was a form of emancipation. In their aspiration to an independent position they were undoubtedly helped by the fact that aristocratic women in France and elsewhere had a greater margin of independence. We remember Mme Châtelet as the mistress of Voltaire and tend to forget that it was she (and her husband; Voltaire lived with them in an amiable *marriage à trois*) and the *Marquis* who maintained and protected him at her country house in Cirey. And how often we see it mentioned that she was a mathematical genius who wrote a commentary on Newton's *Principia Mathematica* which is still treated by the experts with respect? Talent is not sex-bound, but you need the education to develop it. As a girl you had a greater chance in an aristocratic than in a bourgeois family.[14]

A recent book on the Parisian *salons* is by Antoine Lilti.[15] His conclusion is that the *salons were an* upper class affair and so they were. The author has revisionist intentions. According to him the *salon* as portrayed in the conventional view does not exist. There was a myriad of clubs, informal gatherings and societies; none of them was called a *salon*. These societies (Lilti persistently calls them *salons*) were not the hotbeds of the Enlightenment. They were part of that peculiar world

[13] D. Goodman, *The Republic of Letters. A Cultural History of the French Enlightenment* (Ithaca 1994: Cornell University Press), 80.

[14] Ph. Ariès, *Centuries of Childhood* (Harmondsworth 1973: Penguin), tells us that bourgeois started to give special attention to the education of their children, but that applied rather to the sons than to the daughters.

[15] *Le Monde des Salons. Sociabilité et Mondainité à Paris au XVIIIe Siècle* (Paris 2005).

in which a small select group wanted to entertain others and themselves. Lilti also wrote a chapter in order to explode the conventional notion that the *salons* did not meddle into politics, for they did. Very often they were instruments for the promotion of their members.

The revisionist ambition tends to spoil the arguments of a fine book. No *salons*! Why then spend so much attention on the *salons* of Mme Guérin, the Marquise du Deffand, Julie de Lespinasse and of the Baron d'Holbach? Did they not form a distinctive subcategory in the much larger world, which Lilti describes, because they offered discussions on serious subjects next to entertainment?[16] Why then were the *philosophes* invited by members of the highest nobility to join them at dinner? Why did the Duchess of Luxembourg protect Rousseau when he had become an outcast everywhere else and was sought by the police? The answer is that the nobility was interested in their ideas. We might speak of an asymmetrical relationship between the nobility and writers: the nobility had the power, the money and the influence and to a large extent they dictated the code of conduct in the *salons*. Yet the asymmetrical relation also ran in the other direction. Without the *esprit* of the writers and *philosophes* the *salons* would have been a dull affair. Perhaps we could use the metaphor of osmosis to explain the culture of the *salons*. There was a mutual penetration of interests and ideas. Noblemen as well as commoners were interested in the ideas of the Enlightenment and the protected sphere of the *salons* allowed them meeting on terms of equality talking freely about religion, justice and humanity.

Of course politics were discussed, but it was the politics of intrigue. Discussions on constitutional reform did not take place. Lilti gives an impressive account of how the political debate of the seventies hampered and eventually destroyed the sociability of the *salons*. His heroine is Mme Roland who lost her head, because she maintained a *salon* old style in the dangerous times of the Revolution.

Sociability is one of the keywords in Lilti's analysis. It seems to me that net-working was its primary function and the *salons* were

[16] Julie de Lespinasse could not afford to offer her guests dinner, yet het *salon* was very popular.

the ideal instrument for this kind of net-working so promoting the Enlightenment. *Mondanité* is the other keyword. In order to gain access to a *salon* you needed a reputation and you had to conform to a certain code of conduct. That included the maxim never to be dull. The propriety which the code dictated gave a considerable scope to *libertinages* in word and deed. Could it be that Mme Geoffrin added a bourgeois element to the definition of propriety?

Lilti criticises Deni Goodman's *Republic of Letters*, but I still like the central idea of her book. She tells us that the aim of the conversation was to avoid the sharp edges of polemical talk. The abbé Galiani, a Neapolitan diplomat, who had frequented the *salons* in the past but was recalled to Naples (which he considered as a form of exile), wrote a critique of the physiocratic plan of a free grain trade which Turgot, as minister of finance, wanted to put through. Galiani was upset by the sharp tone of Morellet's rejoinder, a government stooge (but also Galiani's friend) who wrote for Turgot. That reaction was not done in the circles of the *salon.* Diderot who took part in the debate pointed out that Turgot's measures might save or destroy the *Ancien Régime.* They did neither: Turgot was fired by the king and the Revolution cleaned up the act.

On the eve of the *convocation* of the *États Généraux* in 1789 discussions were becoming political. Political issues were not discussed in the Republic of Letters. Politics meant the end of the *salons* of the eighteenth-century.

4. Enlightenment and Enlightenments

The culture of the French Enlightenment had a hegemonic influence in Europe that was promoted by the fact that French censorship forced authors to have their books printed in Amsterdam, Geneva or even London. Yet the perception of this French influence was different in each country. The impact of French culture on the Dutch was direct, but the political situation was different. Though the Dutch republic was in a situation of constitutional impasse during the whole of the eighteenth century, the patriciate which ran the republic opted for a closely monitored intellectual freedom and religious tolerance.

The Enlightenment never acquired that semi-illicit character it had in France.

The numerous German courts aspired to become cultural centres as Versailles had been. This was an ironic development, because eighteenth-century Versailles no longer was the cultural centre of France. The imitation underlined the fact that the German courts controlled affairs within their border which was no longer the case in France. I shall discuss the German *Aufklärung* elsewhere. Perhaps the most significant fact of the transmission of French influence was the reaction against it. German writers such as Lessing, the dramatist, started to agitate against the dominance of French models. Understandably there was no love lost between Lessing and Frederick II of Prussia. Lessing became the forerunner of the *Sturm und Drang*, that movement of cultural nationalism which sought to create a genuine German culture.

I shall also deal with Britain in an essay on economic reform. British writers had a great admiration for French polite society as exemplified by the *salons*. However, they were otherwise preoccupied by the problems of an expanding economy and the expansion of the British Empire.

3. Deism, Prospect or Threat?

1. The Inevitability of a Secular View

The title of this essay needs explaining. Deism is the belief that God has created a benevolent natural order and left it to mankind to exploit it. For the deist, miracles, revelation, atonement and the trinity are part of a Christian folklore which cannot be taken seriously. What I mean by threat is that deism was at the end of a slippery slope for Protestants (particularly protestant ministers) who wanted to stick to an orthodox interpretation of the faith, but who on the other hand were susceptible to the ideas of the Enlightenment, which involved a secular world view. Clergymen accused their brethren that they strayed away from the right and narrow path, because they saw the risk of their own interpretation. Tindal, who, at the beginning of the century was accused by Samuel Clarke of deism, wrote:

> If Christianity, as well as Deism, consists in being govern'd by the original Obligation of the moral fitness of Things ... has not the Doctor himself given the Advantage to Deism?[1]

As Clarke was considered not to be safe on the interpretation of the holy trinity, that seems a fair comment. So deism was the common denominator of Protestants who wanted to accommodate their Christian faith to a secular word view. In Britain reaching that common denominator had to be avoided at all costs. Threat means that the secular world view was so attractive that it corroded the traditional story of Christianity. When I use the word inevitable I do not want to suggest that a loss of faith was inevitable. What I mean is that it

---

[1] I. Rivers, *Reason, Grace and Sentiment. A Study of the Language of Religion and Ethics in England 1660-1780,* vol. 1: *Whichcote to Wesley*, vol. 2: *Shaftesbury to Hume* (Cambridge 1991/2001, Cambridge University Press), vol. 2, 80, see also 7.

became very hard for a sophisticated person to take the biblical story at face value. Did miracles really happen or should we interpret them in a symbolic sense? That was the way to go in the nineteenth-century and some eighteenth-century Protestants were prepared to go that way, but many others were stuck in the middle between the biblical story and secularism. In catholic countries the clergy left no room for any form of accommodation. They insisted (and insist) that saints are the intermediaries between God and man. Gibbon took a strong view of this kind of 'superstition'. He wrote:

> The sublime and simple theology of the primitive Christians was gradually corrupted; and the MONARCHY of heaven, already clouded by metaphysical subtleties, was degraded by the introduction of a popular mythology, which tended to restore polytheism.[2]

Obviously Gibbon referred to the worship of saints, but he also wrote about metaphysical subtleties and accordingly he was accused of being a deist. The prospect of deism can be dealt with by a reference to Lessing. His theodicy predicted that deism would become the faith of civilised Europe.

Even in the easy going climate of eighteenth-century opinion it came as a bit of a shock that the cosmologists had constructed a cosmos which could run as a machine and which could do without the intervention of God (Newton, who was not so sure that it could, was an exception). So the Enlightenment in a sense is the attempt to introduce this scientific outlook in human affairs. The philosophers of the Enlightenment are still reputed to have been unbelievers. Those historians who write about the eighteenth century know better, but the label still sticks. However, only a small group of them were atheists. In France it was the small group that convened in the *salon* of Baron d'Holbach that openly though discretely confessed that

[2] E. Gibbon, *The History of the Decline and Fall of the Roman Empire* (London 1995: Penguin), D. Womersley ed., vol. II, ch. 28, 95-96. See on the controversy J.G.A. Pocock, *Barbarism and Religion*, vol. 5: *Religion: the First Triumph* (Cambridge 2010: Cambridge University Press), 313ff.

Samuel Clarke

they did not believe in any God. The majority of the philosophers in France and elsewhere remained Christians, but they refused to accept that God could interfere with their personal lives and they no longer believed in the system of eternal punishment or reward.

But atheism did become a buzz-word in the eighteenth century. It was used to accuse your opponent no longer of heresy but of something much worse: atheism. Spinoza was the principal victim of this use of atheism. There are basically two ways to interpret his philosophy. According to what we might call a structuralist interpretation, Spinoza made a penetrating assessment of the new type of knowledge which the scientific revolution had procured and lifted it to a metaphysical level. According to the other interpretation, Spinoza was a mystic who showed how to get closer to God.

The paradox of his reputation is that he could have become the founding father of the Enlightenment, but owing to Pierre Bayle he did not. According to Bayle, Spinoza was a pantheist who believed that every object on this earth is God. A pantheist in those days was a synonym for an atheist. So Spinoza earned the reputation of being an arch atheist. And, as Paul Vernière has shown, that was how eighteenth-century Frenchmen regarded Spinoza and even those who bothered to read him, such as Voltaire and Diderot, did not see him as their ally.[3] The cliché which Hume produced of Spinoza in his *Treatise* is the best proof that he never read Spinoza.

Only in the German countries did Spinoza's message get across. Writing a review of Jacobi's works, Hegel saw the importance of Spinoza as a philosopher. Now, Hegel remarked, it is time to go beyond Spinoza.[4] Lessing's prospect of deism was the outcome of his reading of Spinoza.

2. *Natural Religion in England and Scotland*

Atheism was not an issue in eighteenth-century Britain, deism was. John Leland defined the deist as a person who did not believe in revelation. He wrote:

> The name of Deists, as applied to those who are no friends to revealed religion, is said to have been first assumed about the middle of the sixteenth century, by some gentlemen in France and Italy, who were willing to cover their opposition to the Christian revelation by a more honourable name than that of Atheists.[5]

---

[3] P. Vernière, *Spinoza et la Pensée Française avant la Révolution* (Paris 1953: P.U.F), 2 vols, vol. 2.

[4] T. Pinkard, *Hegel a Biography* (Cambridge 2000, Cambridge University Press), 384.

[5] J. Leland, *A View of the Principal Deistical Writers* (London 1766: Longman & Dodsley). There was a lot of confusion about the right definition of the deist. Clarke in his *Discourse Concerning the Being and Attributes of God* (1704) distinguished four types of deists: (in the phrasing of L.Dupré), 1. Those who believe in the existence of an eternal, intelligent being that created a certain quantity of matter and motion without concerning itself with its development or government; 2. Those who believe in the providence of God but not in divinely sanctioned moral obligations; 3. Those who believe in God's moral commands but not in immortality; 4. Those who believe in the Providence of God, moral obligations and immortality, but not in revelation. [L.Dupré, *The Enlightenment,*

The suggestion of Leland is of course that deism is a shield for the atheist, but if we look at the list of writers, which Leland discusses, amongst others, Lord Herbert of Chesbury, Tindal, Hobbes, Shaftesbury, Hume and Lord Bolingbroke, all of them believed in revelation except Hume. However, Hume denied that he was a deist and that makes sense, because he did not believe in a benevolent natural order. Chesbury and Tindal might qualify as deists. They believed in revelation, but their belief must have been too heterodox, according to Leland. The point of Leland's –surprisingly courteous– criticism was that their ideas might inspire others to become deists.

Deism was a threat to any orthodox Christian, certainly if he had any liberal leanings to the interpretation of the Scripture. In 1675 Bishop John Wilkins' *Of the Principles of Natural Religion* was published. In it he pleaded for an accommodation of religion and science, but accommodation was the problem. The major point of contention was God's providence, and did He give signs of his intentions by way of miracles? God's providence was registered in the biblical story of the Old and the New Testament and certain episodes of this story were impossible in the light of natural science. Some, like Leland, stuck to the story in its entirety; others were willing to make concessions by viewing these episodes as the allegories of a deeper divine wisdom. The chief bone of contention was the miracles. In 1749 Conyers Middleton published his *A Free Inquiry into the Miraculous Powers Which are Supposed to have Subsisted in the Christian Church, from the Earliest Age, through Several Successive Centuries: By Which it is Shewn that We have no Sufficient Reason to Believe, upon the Authority of the Primitive Fathers, that any Such Powers were Continued to the Church, after the Days of the Apostles.* I have quoted Middleton's title in full, because it contains his message in all its splendour. Only the miracles which Jesus performed are real. Those that are mentioned in the Old Testament are fables and the Catholic Church has been in-

243]. According to Clarke only the fourth kind are real deists. Like Leland Clarke emphasizes revelation (and not providence). Belief in revelation decided whether someone was a deist or not. A generation after Clarke, Conyers Middleton perfectly fitted Clarke's portrait of the real deist.

venting them since the early days of the Church. His *Inquiry* created quite a stir. The year before in 1748, Hume had published his *Philosophical Essays Concerning Human Understanding* (since called *Enquiry Concerning Human Understanding*). In the essay on *Miracles* Hume wrote that *all* miracles are improbable and impossible. He wrote in *My Own Life*:

> On my return from Italy, I had the mortification to find all England in a ferment, on account of Dr. Middleton's Free Enquiry, while my performance was entirely overlooked and neglected.[6]

Given the temper of the time, the arguments of an infidel were less important than the words of a divine (who aspired to be a bishop and never became one). Middleton struck a sensitive nerve: which miracles should a true believing Christian accept as genuine and which should he discard? The discussion on this issue started with Tillotson and by no means finished with Middleton.

It is hard to understand in retrospect the fuss, which Edward Gibbon created with chapters 15 and 16 of his *History of the Decline and Fall of the Roman Empire*. In them he told the story of the early Christians and their sufferings. In his *Vindication* (his answer to his critics) Gibbon had a field day in demonstrating that his handling of the sources was greatly superior to that of his critics, but there was one critic, Dr Watson, who went to the root of the problem, which antagonized Gibbon's critics. He noted the distinction, which Gibbon made between God as the primary cause of the emergence of Christianity and the secondary causes, which explain the rise of early Christianity. And he explained that Gibbon's treatment negated God as the primary cause of life. Gibbon answered Watson courteously and wrote that he was glad that Watson owned "that I have expressly allowed the full and irresistible weight of the *first* great cause of the success of Christianity" and so "The only question which remains

[6] D. Hume, "My Own Life", *Essays Moral, Political and Literar,* (Indianapolis 1987: Libert/*Classics*), E.F. Miller ed., xxxiv. When he wrote this in 1776, Hume had the satisfaction that Middleton's *Free Inquiry* was more or less forgotten, while his had risen on the scale of estimation.

Conyers Middleton

between us, relates to the *degree* of the weight and effect of those secondary causes".[7] The point is of course that as soon as you make the distinction between the signs of God's providence and the documentary evidence the weight falls to the latter. While Watson regarded the activities of the early Christians as the sure signs of God's providence, Gibbon reduced sacred to ecclesiastical history. He painfully demonstrated the difficulties of the divines who wanted to use documentary evidence to restore the terms of sacred history.

Compared to the seventeenth century, religious disputes did not unsettle the social order. The religious polemics only ruffled the surface of a complacent attitude towards religion. Isabel Rivers discusses theological and moral opinions in the seventeenth and eighteenth

[7] E. Gibbon, "Vindication", *The History of the Decline and Fall of the Roman Empire*, vol. III, app. 3, 1156-1157.

century under three headings: grace, reason and sentiment.[8] All three could be divisive, but the *latudinarians* of the Anglican Church managed to create a climate of opinion, which was hospitable to toleration. Natural religion was a powerful concept. It could be used to deny Revelation, but it could also be used to support traditional religion. Joseph Butler gave an authoritative statement of this interpretation in his *Analogy of Religion Natural and Revealed to the Constitution and Course of Nature* (1736). He maintained that our knowledge of the natural order supports God's revelation. That was typically the message of a latudinarian clergyman.

All three sources of religion together -grace, reason and sentiment- were kept together in the Anglican Church. The Tudor monarchs Henry VIII and Elisabeth meant it to be a broad church that would absorb doctrinal differences. That *latitudinarian* aspect of the Church determined the attitudes and beliefs of its members in the eighteenth century. Grace meant that Christians had a special contract with God and it certainly helped that the thirty nine articles, which were established in 1562, were an odd bundle of doctrines and within limits people could read in them what they wanted. Obviously Grace could inspire an egotistic and rebellious attitude. Reason meant common sense and the spirit of moderation, it could also be claimed as an exclusive right to use Reason by the deist or the atheist to judge divine matters. Anglicans were convinced that sentiment could inspire people to do well. Isaac Watts, a popular preacher, told church goers to cultivate sentiment. Rivers writes about his *Doctrine of the Passions*:

The relation between reason and the passions or affections (the terms are used synonymously by Watts) must be understood. In the *Doctrine of the Passions* they are described as 'those sensible emotions of our whole nature, both soul and body, which are occasioned by the perception of an object according to some special properties that belong to it'; they are 'of a mixed nature, belonging partly to the soul, or mind, and partly to the animal body, that is, the flesh and blood'.[9]

---

[8] I. Rivers, *Reason, Grace and Sentiment,* vol. 1.

[9] I. Rivers, *Reason, Grace and Sentiment,* vol. 1, 188.

One can almost replace Watt's name by that of Hume, indicating how widespread the notion was that experience is primarily a matter of perception and sentiment, which after the primary experience we then start to process in our mind or soul.

Toleration was an age old concept, but it seems to me that Locke imported the Dutch idea of toleration into England. It meant that Protestants of different beliefs should respect each other. Catholics were excluded from toleration, but they were suffered ("gedogen" is the untranslatable Dutch word) to worship in private. After William and Mary became King and Queen, in England and Scotland two state churches were established, the Presbyterian Kirk in Scotland, the Anglican Church in England. In England an attempt was made to include dissenters within the state church by way of *comprehension*, but the attempt failed. So the dissenters (to call all the Independents, nonconformists, Quakers etc by this generic name) stayed outside the Anglican Church and so could not hold public office and could not have access to the universities of Oxford and Cambridge. Otherwise they fully participated in public life and founded their own academies where you could get a much better education than in either of the two universities.

Among the dissenters John Wesley was a paradoxical figure. He remained a loyal member of the Anglican Church, but he blazed the trail for what came to be called the Methodist church in the nineteenth century. The Methodists came to emphasize grace and sentiment within their religious communities and for them the doctrinal implications of secularization became a secondary concern.

Rivers' volume one is on theological opinions and volume two deals with moral philosophy. The test of the impact of a secular world view on religion manifests itself in moral theory. The third Earl of Shaftesbury set the tone for eighteenth-century moral philosophy. In his set of essays called *Charackteristics* he made an argument for the combination of sentiment and civility. Francis Hutcheson, an influential professor in Glasgow, did much to fashion a new moral philosophy, which originated in Scotland. Thomas Reid, Dugald Stewart and, of course, the two luminaries David Hume and Adam Smith designed a moral philosophy which, in its broadest outline, meant that it was useful and pleasant for people to work together and promote by their behaviour the new market economy. Adam Smith frowned upon the use of the concept of utility by his friend Hume, but he used it himself in his *Wealth of Nations* as a matter of course. Hume gave a full explanation to Horace's *utile et dulce* in his *Inquiry Concerning the Principles of Morals* (1751). The Scottish school of common sense also used the principle of utility and its teaching became very influential in the colleges of the new American republic. In England of course Jeremy Bentham set his mark on nineteenth-century society and politics with his school of utilitarianism, but perhaps the most evident sign that the secular view had prevailed at the end of the eighteenth century was William Paley's *The Principles of Moral and Political Philosophy* (1785). He developed a kind of utilitarianism under Christian wings. To be a Christian is not only the road to salvation, but turns the Christian into a useful citizen. John Stuart Mill wrote scornfully that Paley was a man "who, whatever principle of morals he professed, seems to have had no object but to insert it as a foundation underneath the existing set of opinions ethical and political".[10] That may be so, but the fact that Paley could incorporate his brand of utilitarianism within the Anglican Church was not only a credit to the accommodating strength of that church but also to the power of the new secular world view.

In Scotland the *moderates* were the counterpart of the *latitudinarians* in the Anglican church. Their position was very different from that of the Anglican clergy. In alliance with the Scottish elite and the protection of the most powerful nobleman in Scotland, the Duke of Argyle, they acquired control over the Kirk and the University of Edinburgh. Richard Sher writes about them:

> As men of letters, the Moderate literati of Edinburgh were not so radical or innovative as many of their continental counterparts, but in their "moderate" way they were as enlightened and *engagés*

[10] J.S. Mill, "Whewell on Moral Philosophy" (1852), *Collected Works*, vol. X, 173.

> as Voltaire and Diderot, and they were considerably more successful than most European *philosophes* at institutionalizing their values during their own lifetimes.[11]

Whether the majority of continental philosophers were more radical than their Scottish counterparts remains open for debate. I, at least, have argued that politically they were conservatives. As to innovation it seems to me that David Hume and Adam Smith have an equal claim to being innovative. However, the importance of this quotation is in its last sentence. The secret of what we now call the Scottish Enlightenment is that the *moderates* were active modernizers and this may explain why Scotland took the lead in moral philosophy. Scotland was relatively poor and backward in its economic development. Given the fact that Scotland had a better system of education than England, Scottish intellectuals, clergymen in the first place, were keen on exploiting new possibilities within a larger Britain. The threat of deism was largely ignored in Scotland. And theological discussions in eighteenth-century Britain as a whole were intense and often hostile but did not lead to religious persecution. Deism was a threat in the eye of the beholder but that did not prevent the critic of deism to accept a morality which was secular in its consequences, if not in its form.

3. French Anticlericalism and Voltaire's Theism

If many protestant clergymen in Europe tended to keep an open mind about the Enlightenment, the Catholic Church was a determined opponent of anything which had to do with the Enlightenment. You could use the Index, that register of books, which the Curia forbade Catholics to read, as a panorama of the Enlightenment. Often, given their point of view, you can understand the decisions of the Curia, but often their decisions were inspired by petty motives as in the case of Montesquieu's *De l'Esprit des Lois.*

[11] R. Sher, *Church and University in the Scottish Enlightenment. The Moderate Literati of Edinburgh* (Princeton 1985: Princeton University Press), p. 328.

The position of the eighteenth-century French church was a disastrous one. At the insistence of Louis XIV pope Clemens XI issued the *Bulla Unigenitus* (1713) in which the doctrines of the Jansenists were condemned. The bull led to a quarrel between the parliaments, which took the side of the Jansenists, and the French king, who in vain tried to put the bull into effect. It led furthermore to a running battle between the Jesuits and the Jansenists and both parties had their laic and clerical supporters. The Jansenists believed in predestination. God in his infinite wisdom had decided to divide mankind in the doomed and the blessed. The Jesuits believed in free will. Voltaire, Diderot and many other *philosophes*, had been educated by the Jesuits and someone, like Diderot, felt a deep seated antipathy for the philosophy of Pascal, one of the luminaries of the Jansenists, but they were the persecuted underdogs and they lived at least according to their strict interpretation of virtue. So in practice the Jansenists had to be tolerated and in the end pope Clemens XIV abolished the Jesuit order in 1771.

The conflict soured the climate of opinion in France and gave rise to anticlericalism among the *philosophes.* Furthermore many clergymen were cruel in their decisions and hypocritical in their behaviour and – even worse– they often appeared plainly ridiculous. So the discerning public laughed heartily at the monks who fined a couple for sleeping together during their bridal night, because they had violated the *ius primae noctis* of the monks.

However, if the *philosophes* were anticlerical in their attitude to the Church (though discretely; you might expect a rich living from the Church) they were for the greater part not atheists. Holbach and his friends were atheists and pure materialists. Holbach drew his inspiration from a curious document: Jean Meslier's Will. This village pastor wrote a withering indictment against the Church and its doctrines. Holbach had it translated under the title *Le Bon Sens du Curé Jean Meslier Suivi de Son Testament.* Holbach and his circle transformed this bitter criticism into a genteel system of order. Lilti maintains that Holbach's notion of sociability was derived from the symbiosis between the nobility and the *philosophes* Writing about the Holbach's notion Lilti observes:

> La théorie de la sociabilité développée par d'Holbach, loin de défendre l'autonomie d'un espace social particulier et égalitaire, s'efforce d'asseoir l'ensemble de l'ordre social, avec ses distinctions de rang et d'état, sur des principes de sociabilité et d'utilité sociale.[12]

This is, I think, an important observation. When we compare the works on moral philosophy by Holbach, Condillac and Helvétius (among others) with their British counterparts the French works remain very abstract and as soon as we try to visualize the actual society to which they were to be applied, they refer to the small world of the *salons,* while Hume wrote for the much larger world of commercial society.

The group of atheists was only small. Most upper class Frenchmen and most *philosophes* felt themselves to be Christians, but they held to a kind of indifferent Christian belief. Voltaire's belief is representative even though he was no Christian. As a young man he wrote of God: "Je ne suis pas chrétien, mais c'est pour t'aimer mieux.[13]

However, the spokesman for the religious feelings of many of the *philosophes* was Rousseau. He combined faith and humanism in eloquent terms. In his *Profession du Foi du Vicaire Savoyard* he wrote:

> J'adore la puissance suprême et je m'attendris sur ses bienfaits. Je n'ai pas besoin qu'on m'enseigne ce culte, il m'est dicté par la nature elle même.[14]

And in his answer to Christophe de Beaumont's *Mandement,* in which the archbishop of Paris had condemned the *Émile,* Rousseau proudly maintained:

---

[12] A. Lilti, *Le Monde des Salons,* 216.

[13] R. Pomeau, *La Religion de Voltaire* (Paris 1969: Nizet), 464.

[14] J.J. Rousseau, "Émile ou l'Éducation", *Oeuvres Complètes* (Paris 1969), IV, 583.

> Monseigneur, je suis Chrétien et sincèrement Chrétien, selon la doctrine de l'Évangile. Je suis Chrétien, non comme un disciple des Prêtres, mais comme un disciple de Jesus-Christ.[15]

We all remember Voltaire's slogan *Écrasez l'infâme*, meaning the Catholic clergy, and he pursued them relentlessly. But he also said that if the Christian churches had not existed they should have been invented. He was acutely aware that the Church and churches in general were important instruments of social control among a population that was not touched by the Enlightenment.

In his *Siècle de Louis XIV* he accepted the Catholic Church as a national institution provided that its clergy would be broadminded enough to tolerate all kinds of religious belief. In his *Essai sur les Moeurs* he maintained that civilisations outside the Christian world had developed such a kind of broad minded theism in which believers had their beliefs in one God in common.[16] Voltaire's theism is a special kind of deism. The God of deism was remote, but Voltaire needed a personal relationship to his God and perhaps in this need he was not alone. It strikes me that Hume denied that he was a deist, but he did not call himself an atheist either. It is as if he felt himself too civilised for that. Could it be that he had the same kind of relationship to God as Voltaire? He did not need a God to help him or to explain the universe. Perhaps he felt that the belief in one God gave an extra, almost aesthetic, quality to the meaning of life. He was, as I have described him, an agnostic theist.[17]

4. *Deism in Germany*

In the German speaking countries Spinoza *was* read. He appealed first of all to Protestants who saw nature as a mystery they wanted to understand. Many theologians of course condemned Spinoza's writings but on the whole these were well read. One of the critics was Christian Wolff, a very influential theologian, who incorporated

[15] J.J. Rousseau, "Lettre à C.de Beaumont", *O.C.*, IV, 960.

[16] J.G.A. Pocock, *Barbarism and Religion*, vol. 2: *Narratives of Civil Government* (Cambridge 1990: Cambridge University Press), p. 107.

[17] F.L. van Holthoon, *Hume, Leven en Werk* (Kampen 2009: Klement), 108.

a Spinozist element in his rationalist interpretation of the Christian religion. *Aufklärung* meant the duty to find God through Reason. That form of rationalism does not seem totally dissimilar to Spinoza's notion of God.

In the last quarter of the century many intellectuals, Jacobi, Mendelssohn, Goethe and Schiller among them, were inspired by Spinoza's view of the universe and man's position in it. From the point of view of this essay Gottlob Ephraim Lessing is the most interesting writer and *Nathan der Weise* and *Die Erziehung des Menschengeslechts* show how deeply he was influenced by Spinoza's philosophy. In his pithy style he described the blessings of ecumenical tolerance and in *Die Erziehung* he formulated a kind of theodicy in which deism would prevail. When in England deism was a position, which had to be avoided at all costs, in Lessing's view deism would become the creed of all civilised human beings.

Lessing was a loyal citizen, but Frederick II did not like him. The reason was simple. Frederick was an enthusiastic supporter of the French enlightenment. Lessing pleaded for a national literature. He felt that the German writers should not slavishly imitate the French. There is one aspect in Lessing's writings, which shows that we are leaving the era of the Enlightenment behind. His *Erziehung* has a dynamic element, which reminds one of Condorcet's *Esquisse.* Man can move forward and will move forward in the course of human progress. In this Lessing moved away from the Enlightenment and helped to establish the *Sturm und Drang* period in the German speaking countries.

So you could say that the prospect of deism was that it would triumph in the nineteenth century and would turn Christianity into a kind of superior humanism. But what kind of triumph was it really? If we can only rely on God's providence in general, but cannot expect any help from Him in our personal lives, how much solace can we derive from his Presence? That was the basic worry of eighteenth-century Christians. Since the nineteenth century it turned an increasing number of Christians into agnostics and atheists.

5. *Happiness*

Ever since I was a student I kept a happy memory of Carl Becker's *The Heavenly City of the Eighteenth-Century Philosophers.*[18] His thesis is that the philosophers of the Enlightenment needed to replace their Christian beliefs by the notion of an earthly paradise that guaranteed happiness in this world. As a historical explanation of the Enlightenment, Becker's thesis cannot be accepted. Few philosophers of the Enlightenment (including the *philosophes*) were prepared to give up their Christian beliefs and become atheists and Becker underestimates the scepticism, which is also an integral part of the Enlightenment. On the other hand these philosophers accepted the idea that the moral rules should be man made. So the question remains with what would you replace the beliefs and traditions of Christianity in this wholly secular world of human transactions: with the promotion of happiness here on earth?

In this respect the *philosophes* as visitors to the *salons* contributed little that could be useful to later generations. Robert Mauzi has described the notions of happiness in eighteenth-century France and sums these up in three aspects:

1. "La recherches des équilibres" between nature, human society, and reason.[19]

2. Happiness means a "sentiment vif de l'existence"[20]

3. "Les réflexions sur le bonheur au XVIIIe siècle, sont toujours fondées sur l'équivoque."[21]

Balance, sentiment and ambivalence: these three notions contain the French ideal of civilised behaviour in the *salons.* It meant finding the right balance between the traditions of church and state and intellectual freedom. The quest for this balance generated a lot of ambivalence. Perhaps the most original element of the French Enlightenment

---

[18] (New Haven 1932: Yale University Press); see also R.O. Rockwood, *Carl Becker's Heavenly City Revisited,* (Hamden Conn. 1968: Archon).

[19] R. Mauzi, *L'Idée du Bonheur dans la Littérature et la Pensée Française au XVIIIe Siècle* (Paris 1960: Colin), 64.

[20] R. Mauzi, *L'Idée du Bonheur,* 649.

[21] R. Mauzi, *L'Idée du Bonheur,* 657.

was the cultivation of vivid emotions. That inspired the sociability of the *salons*, so much admired in and outside France. Talleyrand is supposed to have said that "celui qui n'a pas vécu avant 1789 ne connaît pas la douceur de vivre."[22] That 'douceur de vivre' applied to a very small group. And Frenchmen after the revolution of 1789 had to invent that 'douceur de vivre' again under very different circumstances.

Becker's notion cannot apply to the English or the Scots. Theologians felt the threat of a godless world and named it deism. But the Anglican Church was hospitable enough to absorb the effects of modernization. It seems to me that the Scottish moderates managed to cushion these effects even better. And yet in both cases theologians and writers in general relied on 'custom' (as Hume called the complex of traditional experience in his *Treatise*) to be able to believe that change could not disrupt that traditional order. Hume accepted the possibility of a godless world with equanimity. Perhaps he would have been shocked to learn that social change would wipe out the world he was accustomed to.

Lessing presented deism as the prospect of the values the modern world would accept: freedom, tolerance and justice. He was the true prophet of things to come, at least in the sense that human beings must accept these values (adding that of democracy to it) in order to live together in peace and happiness and prosper.

[22] A. Lilti, *Le Monde des Salons*, 41; if he said it like this. Guizot has a different version.

4. The Nature of Buffon

1. A Fixed World

In his *Histoire Naturelle et Particulière* Buffon maintains that the original scheme of nature is God's work. Jacques Roger comments that for us it is difficult to understand Buffon's meaning in this case, because we are so used to think in evolutionary terms that the notion of a fixed world is foreign to us.[1]

Indeed Buffon inherited a view of a fixed world that did not allow for any alterations in the original scheme. That notion started to lose its credibility in the eighteenth century, because evidence pointed to the fact that the earth had had a history of development and decay. According to *Genesis* God had created the world as a finished product in six days with all the animals and plants. Later, early in the Christian era, the story of *Genesis* was translated into metaphysical terms and so the doctrine of *The Great Chain of Being* emerged. Arthur Lovejoy gave his 'William James Lectures' on this theme, and his series of lectures in book form became famous. The neo-platonists fused Plato's notion of *plenitude* with Aristotle's idea of *continuity*: everything which could exist would exist. *Plenitudo* means that God had filled his Creation with plants and animals as he saw fit. The notion not only explained the diversity of Creation, but also gave a justification for the fact that the Creation was not perfect in its details. The reason given was that, in order to keep the Creation perfect as a universal phenomenon, there had to be defects in its details. This was an elegant explanation of good and evil as an expression of God's will. *Continuity* meant that all the species together constituted a hierarchical order from the smallest insect to man on the top of the ladder. So *The Great Chain of Being* represented an order where all animals and plants had

[1] J. Roger, *Buffon. A Life in Natural History* (Ithaca 1997: Cornell University Press), S.L. Bonnefoi vert, L.P. Williams ed., 297.

Buffon

their fixed place within the universe. The doctrine bears the stamp of Plato's philosophy that what we mortals see are the shadows of a transcendent ideal reality, but it also refers to Aristotle's concept of final causality. Applied to *The Great Chain* of being, it means that every creation has its own final cause or, in other words, its unique function and destiny. As does creation as a whole.

The Great Chain of Being was such a powerful doctrine that it captivated the minds of generations of commentators on the story of Creation. And when a wayward scholar would question it, the Church authorities would be quick to intervene, as Buffon discovered when, in 1753, the doctors of the Sorbonne reproached him for his deviations from the true story.

However, how could anyone maintain that the world was fixed in its present mode from the beginning? Bones of extinct animals had been found, and then there were the shells high up in the Alps. It seemed evident that the earth went through a phase when most of its surface had been covered with water. Now the story of the Deluge could explain the inundation, even though it was hard to imagine that a story typical of the Middle East could apply to the globe as a whole. However, the shells suggested a considerable lapse of time. How would you explain that interval?

Critical was the computation of the earth's existence, according to the Bible, since creation. According to that computation the earth could be 5000 years, perhaps 8000 years old, but not more. All the evidence pointed too a much longer period in which the earth reached its present shape. Buffon's estimates differed wildly. According to one estimate the earth was 75.000 years old, according to another 2.993.280 years (note the precise numbers). These two estimates show of course a sensational difference, but in both cases they could not be brought into agreement with the biblical story. The earth was assumed to be much older and secondly - and this is crucial – the earth had slowly evolved to reach its present shape.

How can you maintain, Voltaire wrote in his *Dictionnaire Philosophique*, that the Great Chain of Being is without gaps? Why is there no intermediate creature between ape and man? And how do you know that all possible gaps are actually filled? Voltaire ridiculed the idea of *continuity*.[2] All these considerations taken together show us that the doctrine of the Great Chain of Being was starting to lose its hold on the philosophers of the Enlightenment.

2. Buffon, Entrepreneur in Natural Science

Georges-Louis Leclerc was born in Montbard, a village near Dijon. He came from a well-established bourgeois family. His father bought a seat in the parliament of Dijon and so became one of the notables in Burgundy. He bought the estate of Buffon with all the feudal dues attached to it. His son would build a castle on the property and develop a park around the house, and since 1734 Georges Leclerc started to call himself de Buffon. He was still a bourgeois, but he clearly aspired to an aristocratic lifestyle. Later the King made him Count de Buffon to honour his achievements for France. However, Buffon remained

[2] A.O. Lovejoy, *The Great Chain of Being. A Study of the History of an Idea* (New York 1960: Harper), 252.

a hardworking bourgeois. He erected an office in his park and it was there that he wrote his works.

He went to a Jesuit school and his teachers cultivated his love for mathematics. Afterwards he went to the law school of Dijon. Why he made that choice is not known. He never practiced as a lawyer, but it benefited him in another way. He made friends for a lifetime. Among them there was the Abbé de Blanc whom we recognize as the translator of Hume's *Political Discourses*; Charles de Brosses, an opponent of Voltaire, (Buffon shared Charles' disgust of the man), and Richard de Ruffey who became a powerful magistrate in Dijon and could take care of Buffon's interests, particularly when Buffon was away in Paris.

Buffon started his writing career with a paper on game theory. That essay earned him a membership of the *Académie des Sciences*, but he did not pursue his mathematical exercises. His attention to science was too encyclopaedic and too practical to be satisfied with pursuing mathematical speculations. His attention shifted to the general view of nature. He became, you might say, the entrepreneur in a museum of curiosities which became very popular in the eighteenth century.[3] However, Buffon turned this encyclopaedic bric à brac into a systematic analysis of nature in which cosmology, mineralogy, geology and biology, came into play.

Buffon also put his science into practice. The acting minister for the French navy asked him whether it was possible to cultivate oak wood that was strong enough to build men of war. So Buffon planted a forest of oak trees on his estate. He also had built a smelting furnace and he was the first in France to experiment with the use of cokes in the smelting process. Commercially his furnace was not a great success, but the furnace allowed him to use red hot iron balls to measure the cooling process of these balls. He used his experiments to compute the age of the earth.

By nature a late riser, he forced himself to be at work early in the morning. He worked until half past five in the afternoon and then went to visit his maîtresse, at least before he married. In the summer he stayed

[3] A famous one, Teylers museum in Haarlem was founded in 1778.

in Montbard and during the winter he participated in the intellectual life of Paris. He did not frequent the *salons*: sober and practical, he had no use for lightweight conversation.

In 1739 the Intendant of the Royal Botanical Garded died, and the King and his minister decided that Buffon was the ideal man to replace him. His appointment was the beginning of a brilliant career as director of the Royal Botanical Garden, which still exists as the *Jardin des Plantes* in Paris. He was active in acquiring special collections of plants, he was busy constructing buildings and the most famous outcome of his work as director was the publication of his *Histoire Naturelle*. That history established his fame.

The first series appeared between 1749 and 1767 in 5 volumes; the second series followed between 1770 and 1782 in 9 volumes; and the *Histoire Naturelle* was completed with a supplement of 9 volumes. All these volumes were published in *quarto* and the fact emphasizes the daunting size of Buffon's literary production. Buffon could rely on many co-workers to assist him, but essentially the work was his. It is a mystery to me how the Bourbon kings who had so many able men at their disposal –Turgot was another one – could make such a mess of things.

3. The Histoire Naturelle

How, as an *ignoramus* of the fields in which Buffon worked, can I comment on his major publication? Perhaps I can say something relevant on what nature meant to Buffon. In his first volume we can read this wonderful sentence:

> Pourquoi les ouvrages de la Nature sont-ils si parfaits? C'est que chaque ouvrage est un tout, & qu'elle travaille sur un plan éternel dont elle ne s'écarte jamais.[4]

This reads as a reverence to the Great Chain of Being and we know that Buffon did his utmost not to antagonize the authorities of the Church. However, his reference to the perfect plan of nature was more than a civil but empty gesture. The Great Chain of *Being* was

[4] De Buffon & Daubenton, *Histoire Naturelle* (Amsterdam 1766), deel 1, iv.

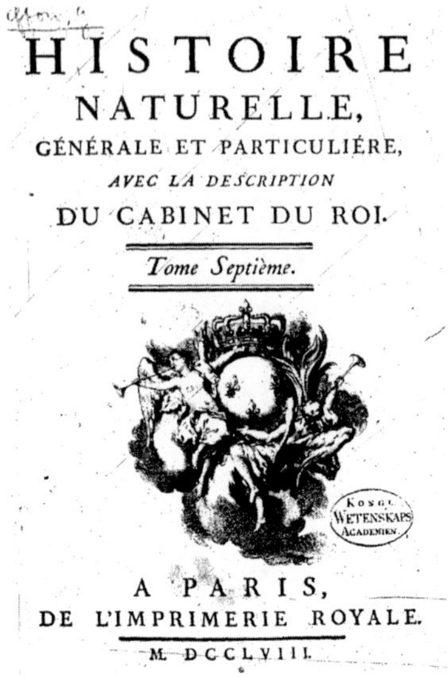
HISTOIRE
NATURELLE,
GÉNÉRALE ET PARTICULIÈRE,
AVEC LA DESCRIPTION
DU CABINET DU ROI.
Tome Septième.
A PARIS,
DE L'IMPRIMERIE ROYALE.
M. DCCLVIII.

his point of departure but, in the course of his analysis the idea of an eternal plan receded into the background. He became more and more interested in the problem of change or flux as he called it. Though he was willing to pacify the authorities where he could, he quietly went his own way.

From the beginning *The Great Chain of Being* did not function for Buffon as a justification for *Genesis.* Having no need for metaphysics, he asked himself what determined the natural order. That order, according to him, is the outcome of a long development, and I have already quoted his computations on the age of the earth.[5]

Why is it that we find shells high up in the Alps, and how is that we discover the remnants of so many extinct species? Buffon was not concerned about the gaps which had occurred in the Great Chain of Being. Instead, he tried to understand why the earth had always re-

[5] The great discrepancy between the estimates may be the result of latent causes that we cannot compute: see Roger, *Buffon,* lxv.

mained in a state of flux, and his concern brought him on the brink of a theory of evolution. When leafing through the volumes of the first series on the Quadrupeds, we notice at first Buffon's exact descriptions and measurements. He measured sizes of animals, their bones and organs, and Daubenton, a member of his family, produced fine engravings of the animals listed.[6] So we get a clear picture of each animal that was discussed. Buffon was highly critical of Linnaeus' ambition to catch nature within the straitjacket of a system. He himself preferred a simple one:

> [C]'est pourquoi nous ne suivrons dans l'Histoire Naturelle & dans la description des animaux quadrupèdes que l'ordre le plus simple & le plus éloigné de toute distribution méthodique; nous commencerons par les animaux domestiques, ensuite viendront les animaux sauvages, & enfin les animaux étrangers.[7]

Buffon's description of animals and plants are imbedded in an elaborate analysis of the origin and development of the earth. That analysis I will deal with in the next paragraph. However it is clear that his history of the earth did not please the doctors of the Sorbonne. But the Sorbonne had to move carefully, because Buffon was an important civil servant whose books were printed at the *Imprimerie Royale* and so had passed the censorship in the name of the King.

In 1751 the Sorbonne made objections to fourteen of Buffon's pronouncements in the first three volumes of his *Histoire Naturelle*. One of these was Buffon's conclusion that truth is a relative notion. Had Buffon forgotten that the truth of the Bible was absolute? Buffon's answer was that he never had wanted to contradict the truth of the Holy Writ. The Sorbonne was very happy with this answer, though it must have been clear to them that he contradicted the biblical story at many points.[8] When his *Les Époques de la Nature* appeared

[6] I have seen the Amsterdam reprint of 1766. I assume that the engravings are the original ones.

[7] Buffon, *Histoire Naturelle* (Amsterdam 1766), dl IV, 62.

[8] See for the exchange of letters J.Lyons & Ph.R. Sloan, *From Natural History to the History of Nature* (Notre Dame 1981: University of Notre Dame Press), 283 ff.

in 1779, there was another exchange of letters. Buffon gave the same answer as in 1751 and admitted openly to others that he could not care less how the Sorbonne reacted to his answer. The Sorbonne, however, triumphantly published also this exchange of letters, but nobody paid any attention to this publication. Nobody took the Sorbonne seriously anymore.

In his private life Buffon behaved as a dutiful son of the Church, but he was hardly a Christian anymore. His *Époques*, his version of the origin of the world and man's role in it, is the ending of a process of fruition in which Buffon did not as such criticize the teaching of the Church, but ignored it. Instead of a God who has created the world, God has become an observer. God had had nothing to do with the creation of the world; at best, He gave it His blessing.

4. Les Époques de la Nature

In a series of "periods," Buffon had formerly speculated on the development of the cosmos and on the problem of the degeneration of animals because of domestication, and had regarded man as another domesticated animal. His view echoed Rousseau's argument in his *Discours de l'Inégalité*, that civilization had corrupted man.[9] Now, in *Les Époques*, in the seventh period, Buffon painted a much more positive prospect of the role of man. Man is seen as the creature that will master nature and turn it to his own use. That prospect makes the *Époques* a document of the Enlightenment. Let me review the periods one by one.

1. *The first period*: The earth comes into existence, because a comet crashed into the sun. Fragments of the sum are launched into space and one of them became planet earth. It started to turn around the sun and it own axis.

The earth in its first existence is a little sun of melted glass, which gradually cools. The cooling process, which, as we have seen, Buffon tried to measure, is the leading theme of the *Époques*. How long did

[9] J. Roger, *Buffon*, 302.

it take before the earth became hospitable to plants and animals, and when will life on earth become impossible again?

2. *The second period*: About 25.000 years after the beginning, mountains started to appear in the course of the cooling process. The earth was still too hot to retain water on its surface.

3. *The third period*: About 37.500 years after the beginning, powerful downpours of rain created seas, which covered most of the surface of the earth, only leaving the mountain peaks dry. Fish, shell-fish now extinct, started to inhabit the seas. The shell-fish became responsible for the rocks of chalk we find at Dover. On the slopes of the mountains animals lived much larger than those of today and they also have become extinct.

When an equilibrium between land and water has been reached, all kinds of sediments are settling down, forming layers of clay and veins of minerals. The discovery of coal makes it clear that during the period there was a lush growth of plants and trees forming organic material.

4. *The fourth period*: This is the period of active volcanoes. And so we now get four kinds of material: glass, chalk, organic material and lava. The volcanoes add to new mineral deposits. Active volcanoes, according to Buffon, are to be found near water and with abundance of water there are many volcanoes. With the retreat of the seas the once active have become dormant.[10]

5. *The fifth period*: About 60.000 years *ab orbe condito* we find elephants in Siberia and North America. The elephant apparently was Buffon's favourite animal. Did he spend on other animals a few pages, the elephant got 70. According to him the elephants had migrated from the Arctic to the tropical zone when the cooling process of the earth made the North inhabitable for elephants.[11]

[10] Buffon was clearly thinking of volcanoes such as the Etna and the Vesuvius, and apparently did not know about active volcanoes in the middle of Java.

[11] Buffon did not know about ice ages. The woolly mammoth was well adapted to life in Siberia and became extinct when the earth was warming up after the last ice age.

Man appears during this period. New species occur, according to Buffon, when an opportunity for their existence occurs. Then organic molecules accumulate to form the species which fills the new niche. Man comes late in the development of the earth, because he has a special mission to fulfil:

> Ainsi nous sommes persuadés, indépendamment de l'autorité des Livres sacrés, que l'homme a été créé le dernier & qu'il n'est venu prendre le sceptre de la Terre que quand elle s'est trouvée digne de son empire.[12]

6. *The sixth period*: The link which connected America and Europe was broken and a breach of the isthmus at Gibraltar connected the Mediterranean lake with the oceans.

7. *The seventh period*: Buffon computed that 168.000 years from the beginning life on earth would end, but perhaps there was no direct cause for alarm, for it could also happen after 7 million years. In the seventh period man is at the centre of things. He has taken possession of the earth:

> [I]l en a pris possession par ses travaux de culture, & l'attachement à la patrie a suivi de très-près les premiers actes de sa propriété: l'intérêt particulier faisant partie de l'intérêt national, l'ordre, la police & les lois ont dû succéder, & la société prendre de la consistance & des forces.[13]

Buffon is telling the story of man as we can read it in Voltaire's *Essai*. What I have not read elsewhere is that he assumes there has been a race of men that in primeval time already had a high level of civilization that since was lost for a long time. Mankind has long been the victim of the barbarism of war and violence, and only slowly we have distanced ourselves from the militaristic empires of the past and

---

[12] Buffon, *Les Époques*, 161. Roger remarks that we should not accuse Buffon of anthropomorphism too quickly, because he may not have meant what he wrote. His reference to the Holy Writ may have been ironic. Now Buffon was not known for his irony and I think the text of his seventh period proves that he had an anthropomorphic view of nature.

[13] Buffon, *Les Époques*, 206.

have chosen for a peaceful cooperation between nations. This was, as we have seen, a favourite theme of the philosophers of the Enlightenment.[14]

Perhaps, Buffon suggests, man's inventive spirit can retard the cooling of the earth, for instance by the intensive use of the new material coal. Man gifted by nature with reason is capable of aiding nature through plant cultivation. The remarkable results thereof can be seen in the Royal botanical Garden.[15] The special breeding programs for animals are another case of man's cooperation with nature. The last sentence of Buffon's book reads:

> Il semble que de tout temps l'homme ait fait moins de réflexions sur les bien que de recherches pour le mal; toute société est mêlée de l'un & de l'autre; & comme de tous les sentiments qui affectent la multitude, la crainte est le plus puissant, les grands talens dans l'art de faire du mal ont été les premiers qui aient frappé l'esprit de l'homme, ensuite ceux qui l'ont amusé ont occupé son cœur, & ce n'est qu'après un trop long usage de ces deux moyens de faux honneur & de plaisir stérile, qu'enfin il a reconnu que sa vraie gloire est la science, & la paix son vrai bonheur.[16]

This is the Enlightenment manifesto of the director of a botanical garden.

5. Buffon and Nature

In the introduction to the set of essays John Lyon and Philip Sloan have published, they suggest that Buffon was much influenced by Leibniz' concept of causality, because he, in accordance with Leibniz's philosophy, did emphasize the real relations between phenomena.[17] This may be so, though I suspect that it was Buffon's pragmatic view of reality which induced him to make this choice. Tracing influences is not always a profitable exercise, because – as in the case of Buffon –

---

[14] Buffon asks himself whether the English are wise in building a colonial empire, cf. *Les Époques*, 212.

[15] Buffon, *Les Époques*, 220.

[16] Boffon, *Les Époques*, 220.

[17] J. Lyon & Ph. R. Sloan, *From Natural History to the History*, 21-22.

it gives no real insight into an author's motive for thinking something out. And why, when the authors see a linkage between Leibniz and Buffon, do they not refer us to Leibniz' concept of sufficient cause? That brings us back to Aristotelian final causality.

According to Lovejoy Leibniz gave a new twist to the notion of final cause. He meant to say that "the thing at all events has *some* reason, that is *logically* grounded in something else which is logically ultimate".[18] So the final cause points to an ultimate thing and that ultimate thing was what Leibniz called a monad. Leibniz's idea of monads express the notion of *plenitude* ans well as of *continuity*. So by a detour we are back at the Great Chain of Being.

It makes sense to start an analysis of Buffon's work with the doctrine of The Great Chain of Being. It looks as if Buffon left the doctrine behind in the course of his work. The fixed world was becoming a world in transition and Buffon's story of the development of the world is not that different from what later geologists would write, except in the details of course. Should we say that Buffon's analysis brought him at the brink of a theory, and perhaps of *the* theory of evolution? We have described Buffon's evolutionary theory, but it differs from Darwin's theory in one fundamental point. For Darwin the struggle for life and the competition between species and of individuals within a species is the engine of evolution. Buffon, however, describes the emergence of nature in which every creature finds its place. Nature to him was what we would now call a gigantic eco-system. And though Buffon did not need God to prove his story, his reference to that order still betrays the Great Chain of Being.

In one respect Buffon had an insight, which is lacking in the work of Darwin. One might say that man as he emerged in the story of the earth stopped evolution in its tracks. Apart from viruses and small insects, the species we know today have not evolved any further. The tiger is not on its way to a new species; in fact, it is almost extinct because of man.

---

[18] A.O. Lovejoy, *The Great Chain of Being*, 146.

Arthur Oncken Lovejoy

There is something else. It is a pity that Buffon did not elaborate his view of the role of man in nature. However, I have the suspicion that he saw nature and man as allies, at least in *Les Époques*.[19] That idea of an alliance would fit in well with the *Enlightened* view of nature.

At this point we must make a *salto mortale*. Johan Huizinga came to the conclusion that the eighteenth-century view of history did not match that of nature and, of course, this is the case.[20] Voltaire's *Essai* and Hume's *Natural History of Religion* have nothing in common with Buffon's story of plants and animals. And yet there is a connexion. Let me point out that connection by referring to Hume's *Treatise of*

[19] He may not always had this rosy opinion. Earlier on he has a remark that man terrorizes wild animals and turns domestic animals into slaves, cf J.Roger, *Buffon*, 233.

[20] J. Huizinga, *Cultuurbeeld en Historiebeeld in de Achttiende-Eeuw* (Groningen 1933: Wolters).

The Great Chain of Being

Human Nature. In book III Hume makes the distinction between artificial and natural virtues. Artificial virtues depend on the prescription of conventional rules about what ought and ought not to be done in society. Natural virtues are a product of the amiable qualities of human beings. Hume made the distinction to argue that artificial virtues would acquire natural qualities in the course of civilization. In his rewriting of this part of the *Treatise* he dropped the distinction.[21] The term 'artificial' had raised adverse comments, because critics were shocked that Hume regarded the rulings they were accustomed to as 'artificial', and Hume felt that he no longer needed the distinction. If conventional rules can become natural, why bother? Hume touched here on an important point, which he then evaded. Like all the phi-

[21] See my *A Dialogue on David Hume, on his Revision of the Treatise of Human Nature* (Amsterdam 2007: Boom), Twelfth Evening, "From Artificial to Natural Virtues, Joining Hutcheson and his School", 128-139.

losophers of the Enlightenment he regarded the conventional morality as natural. Many conventions were absurd or cruel in their eyes, but others they regarded as the cornerstones of a civilized life. All the philosophers saw it as a fact of life, and thus of nature, that the status of a married woman was inferior to that of her husband. We would not regard this at all as a natural rule, and the curious fact is that it took only a small lapse of time to make people aware that it was not. Buffon made his own contribution to this implicit notion of the natural. In a dissertation on puberty he wrote that monogamy was the "natural state of people after puberty".[22] Now monogamy was not evident in the ethnographical accounts of his days nor was it evident in the society in which Buffon moved. What he meant of course was that marriage created the conditions of an orderly life, but the fact that he called it a 'natural state' means that he considered that a self-evident fact.

The link between the view of history and the view of nature in eighteenth-century thought is but a weak one, but it explains how a man such as Buffon, notwithstanding his adventurous thinking, had a very conventional view of human society. Mannheim has made the distinction between traditionalism and conservatism.[23] A conservative tries to maintain an order which he believes is under threat. The traditionalist accepts conventions, because that is how things are and we cannot do without them. Buffon was a traditionalist in some aspects of his thought and so it was with the philosophers of the Enlightenment in general. Their traditionalism marks a watershed between them and conservatives of today and not only them. The watershed applies to modern man in general. Hegel wrote, in his *Die Vernunft in der Geschichte* that, when we become aware that freedom applies to us all, we can protest against it, but the view that only some people are allowed to have it is no longer self-evident.[24]

---

[22] J. Roger, *Buffon*, 168.

[23] K. Mannheim, "Das conservative Denken", *Wissenssoziologie* (Neuwied 1964: Luchterhand), K.H. Wolff ed., 408-508.

[24] W. Kaufmann, *Hegel. A Reinterpretation* (Notre Dame 1978: University of Notre Dame Press), 249.

5. Jean-Jacques Rousseau, an Interpretation

1. Rousseau's Influence

Was Rousseau a philosopher of the Enlightenment or should we regard the man as a pre-romantic whose work was a major influence in the nineteenth century? The trouble is that he was both. I will argue that:

a. The central theme of his political and social thinking was his idea that man is too smart and that the sciences and the arts have created a civilization in which humans cannot be happy. I use the word 'smart' on purpose. Smart means here that we have misused our creative gifts. Rousseau was not against science and art as such. Sciences and the arts could have created a world of harmony and transparent human relations, but they did not.

b. His political and social ideas are not new, but part of the traditional stock of political philosophy.

c. They are, however, transfused by a sensibility that was appreciated by his contemporaries and settled his reputation as the prophet of nineteenth-century revolutionaries.

When his prize-winning essay *Discours sur les Sciences et les Arts* (1750) was published, Rousseau became, as he told us later, a celebrity. What a wonderful paradox to argue that the so-called progress of the arts and the sciences was a mistake. The literate public was soon to be disabused. When Rousseau's second discourse, his *Discours sur l'Inégalité* (1754) was published, it became clear that he meant what he wrote in his first discourse. In a large state such as the French monarchy human relations were out of joint and the civilization, which went with it, was a source of corruption. Rousseau became the persistent critic of the *monde des salons* in which the *philosophes* met and discussed their ideas. Voltaire wrote in the margin of his copy of the second discourse 'ruffian' and 'pitiful'. And in a letter (duly published) he wrote to Rousseau that he had lost the habit of walking on four legs sixty years ago. It was the beginning of a feud, which lasted till Voltaire died in 1778.

Rousseau definitely was an outsider. The Marquise du Deffand wrote to Voltaire in 1764:

> Jean-Jacques m'est antipathique, il remettrait tout dans le chaos, je n'ai rien vu de plus contraire au bon sens que son *Émile*, rien de plus contraire aux bonnes moeurs que son *Héloïse* et de plus ennuyeux et de plus obscur que son *Contrat Social*.[1]

And a year later all Rousseau's acquaintances started to doubt his sanity. Hume had taken Rousseau to England, found lodgings for him and even acquired a pension from the British king. Rousseau responded to Hume's hospitality with hysterical outbursts against him. He accused Hume of wanting to exhibit him as a circus animal. Hume, who was a friendly soul, concluded that "the poor man is absolutely lunatic."[2] And yet such was Rousseau's influence on the reading public that Hume, at that moment minister to the Crown, felt the need to justify his behaviour on paper. In a *Concise and Genuine Account of the Dispute between Mr. Hume and Mr. Rousseau* (also translated in French) he protested his innocence.[3] He had in no way conspired against the poor man. Rousseau had reasons enough to feel persecuted, but in the case of Hume paranoia had taken over. At that time Rousseau was suffering from immense pain. He had a blocked urethra and had to urinate through an inserted reed. But his suffering does not explain his paranoia. Jean Starobinski argues that Rousseau was looking for the transparence of human relations and that he experienced the smallest hitch in his personal relations as an obstacle. As his

[1] J.J. Rousseau, *Oeuvres Complètes* (Paris 1959: Pléiade), vol.1, p. 1545, note attached to Rousseau's *Confessions.*

[2] Hume to Turgot, May 1767, cited by R. Zeretsky & J.T. Scott, *The Philosophers' Quarrel, Rousseau, Hume, and the Limits of Human Understanding* (New Haven 2009: Yale University Press), 197.

[3] Hume and the *philosophes* were worried what Rousseau would write about them in his *Confessions,* his memoirs.

Jean Jacques Rousseau

obstacles, real or imagined, piled up, he became paranoid. Starobinski quotes Rousseau from his letter to the Archbishop of Paris Christophe de Beaumont:

> Je la trouvai dans notre ordre social, qui, de tout point contraire à la nature que rien ne détruit, la tirannise sans cesse, et lui fait sans cesse réclamer ses droits. Je suivis cette contradiction dans ses conséquences, et je vis qu'elle expliquoit seule tous les vices des hommes et tous les maux de la société.[4]

This quotation explains perfectly the chemistry of Rousseau's thinking: because society tyrannises the individual, all he can do is to claim his own rights.

[4] J. Starobinski, *Jean-Jacques Rousseau. La Transparence et l'Obstacle* (Paris 1971: Gallimard), 37. See, for the quotation, "Lettre à Chr. de Beaumont", Rousseau, *Oeuvres Complètes* (Paris 1969: Pléiade), vol. 4, 966-967.

Do Rousseau's ideas belong to the Enlightenment? They do, of course. However wayward those who belonged to the movement of the Enlightenment might think his ideas, they were deeply influential. The secret of his influence is his style of writing. It went straight to the heart of his readers and Rousseau more than any other eighteenth-century writer managed to give meaning to human sentiments. His mastery shows itself in his novel *La Nouvelle Héloïse*. It still is, for all its length, a great novel which even the modern reader will not easily set aside.

Rousseau's political ideas puzzled his eighteenth-century readers, but they had a great influence on the readers of the next century. Henri-Frédéric Amiel (the writer of a long diary) wrote:

> I]l a fait un nouveau style français, le style serré, châti, dense, passionné. En somme, on peut dire que rien de Rousseau ne s'est perdu et que personne n'a influé plus que lui, sur la Révolution française … et sur le XIXe siècle.[5]

And J.L. Talmon wrote that Rousseau was responsible for the *esprit révolutionaire,* which led to totalitarian democracy:

> In the *Discourse on Inequality* he expresses the burning sense of a society that has gone astray. In the *Social Contract* he postulates an exclusively legitimate social system as a challenge to human greatness.[6]

Now, whatever we think of Amiel's and Talmon's explanation of Rousseau's influence, that influence is a fact, but the intriguing question remains why Rousseau's writings were so influential in the nineteenth-century. Rousseau's political ideas appear to be traditional rather than innovative. Rousseau himself denied that he was a revolutionary and he was not a democrat, at least in the modern sense. Part of the object of this essay is to explain the reception of Rousseau's ideas in the nineteenth century.

---

[5] Cited by A. Cobban, *Rousseau and the Modern State* (London 1968), 15.

[6] J.L. Talmon, *The Origins of Totalitarian Democracy* (London 1961: Mercury), 49.

Marquise Du Deffand

2. The Need for a Simple World

Roger Masters writes that the theme of Rousseau's first discourse determines the character of his political thought and indeed the plea for a simple life is at the background of all his writings. At the beginning of his discourse Rousseau writes that we need a revolution "pour ramener les hommes au sens commun".[7] Escaping from the middle ages we went the wrong way. We have used our talents to create a frivolous world:

> Aujourd'hui que des recherches plus subtiles et un goût plus fin ont réduit l'Art de plaire en principes, il règne dans nos moeurs une vile et trompeuse uniformité.[8]

[7] J.J. Rousseau, "Discours sur les Sciences et les Arts", *Oeuvres Complètes* (Paris 1964: Pléiade), vol. 3, p. 6.

[8] J.J. Rousseau, "Discours sur les Sciences et les Arts", *O.C.*, vol.3, p. 8.

But our common sense should make us think back to the time when human beings got together and formed a society.

> L'Image de la simplicité des premiers temps. C'est un beau rivage, paré des seules mains de la nature, vers lequel on tourne incessament les yeux, et dont on se sent éloigner à regret.[9]

Rousseau has got the reputation that he wanted us to get back to nature (Voltaire is responsible for this), but he was thinking of that first stage of human society, when people learnt to live by certain simple rules. Rousseau's logic runs like this: because human nature is intrinsically good the founders of the first society took delight in following the simple rules they had established. In following this logic he is more a follower of Locke than of Hobbes, except that, according to Locke, individuals in the state of nature already follow some implicit rules, which they then formalize while founding a political society. The point of the first *Discours* is that things went wrong since the stage of this primeval society. Man is too inventive in thinking out new things and too smart in applying them.

The first *Discours* was a prize-winning essay for the Academy of Dijon. The Academy had asked whether the sciences and the arts had promoted morality. What did Rousseau mean to say with his negative answer? That eighteenth-century art corrupted manners can be understood (though we do not have to agree with the conclusion), but what about science? Rousseau did not give a clear answer to this. In his discourse on political economy he wants government to disentangle economic relations, which have become too complicated. These relations are -at least in part- the product of scientific inventions. It is impossible for anyone to stop this kind of scientific progress. That scientific progress has made life more complicated is a fact and the fact may have made Rousseau's contemporaries uneasy, not only Rousseau. As a polite gesture he expressed the hope that the Academy could help to restore the proper function of the sciences and the arts. He came to hate his first *Discours*, not because of its tame end, but because it made him famous. His sophisticated public appreciated the paradox that the sciences and the arts

9 J.J. Rousseau, *O.C.*, vol. 3, p. 22.

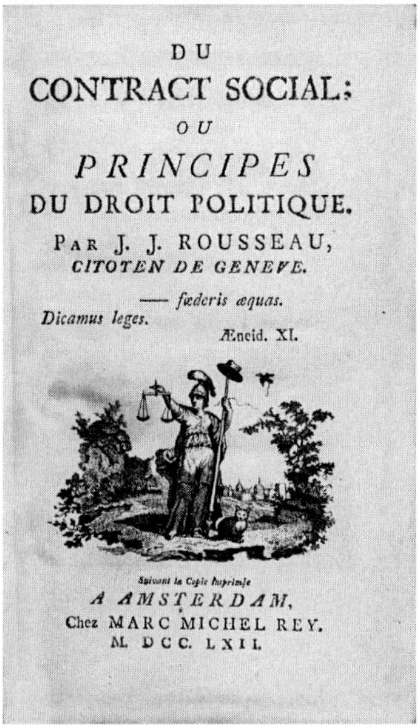
DU
CONTRACT SOCIAL;
OU
PRINCIPES
DU DROIT POLITIQUE.
PAR J. J. ROUSSEAU,
CITOYEN DE GENEVE.
— fœderis æquas.
Dicamus leges.
Æneid. XI.

A AMSTERDAM,
Chez MARC MICHEL REY.
M. DCC. LXII.

could make life too complicated. And perhaps the accusation that the contemporary artificiality of manners destroyed the transparency of human relations struck a cord. Rousseau's appeal to common sense made him acquire unlikely fellows. He also appealed to the philosopher. Let us consult man's direct experience and forget about the metaphysical musings of the human mind. The young Hume wrote in his *Treatise* "that the understanding, when it acts alone … entirely subverts itself, and leaves not the lowest degree of evidence in any proposition, either in philosophy or in common life".[10] Rousseau's appeal to common sense was not in vain. Both writers claimed that our understanding must be based on our sensory experience and not on abstract principles. We cannot discover truth by thinking about it. We need experience as a starting

[10] D. Hume, *A Treatise of Human Nature*, I, 4, vii, 267-268.

point. It is the kind of experience that all human beings can understand, provided they have common sense.[11]

Common sense can mean two things. First, it refers to the common body of knowledge which everybody appreciates as such and, secondly, it defines our capacity to distinguish between the true and the false.[12] Rousseau and Hume agreed that our sensory experience is the starting point of our approach to reality and they certainly disagreed about what constitutes a common body of knowledge. Hume regarded custom as a necessary ingredient of stable human relations and he accepted the rules and customs as they occurred in any society. Rousseau wanted to simplify the prescription for human behaviour and thought that some simple rules were sufficient to guarantee the public order. But his public was dimly aware that things were changing and in retrospect we can confirm that the customary world of both Rousseau and Hume has melted away. Rousseau acted as a kind of seismograph of the Enlightenment. Mauzi has told us that French writers were ambivalent about their feelings of happiness. Rousseau by his appeal to a simple life exploited this ambivalence.

Rousseau's second discourse, the *Discours sur l'Origine et les Fondements de l'Inégalité parmi les Hommes* (1754) was not at all well received and that reaction can be easily understood, for it contained a direct assault on the Ancien Régime, not so much on its regime as on its culture. The *Discours* was dedicated to the Magistrate of the Republic of Geneva, because the town was small and could be well-governed. It was a civil society "d'une grandeur bornée par l'étendue des facultés humaines, c'est-à-dire par la possibilité d'être bien gouvernée."[13]

---

[11] Thomas Reid's name does not appear in the indices of Rousseau's *Oeuvres Complètes*, so he presumably did not read Reid's works, but his idea of common sense is closer to that of Reid than of Hume. For Rousseau and Reid common sense is the gift of immediately grasping the truth; for Hume the common sense world is the outcome of a complicated process of the imagination.

[12] F.L. van Holthoon and D.R. Olson, "Common Sense an Introduction," *Common Sense, the Foundations for Social Science* (Lanham MD 1987: University Press of America), F.L. van Holthoon & D.R. Olson eds.

[13] J.J. Rousseau, "La République de Génève", *Discours sur l'Origine et les Fondemens de l'Inégalité, O.C.*, vol. 3, p. 111.

Jean Starobinski

Those living in great states were less fortunate. For them it was almost impossible to be well-governed. Rousseau wrote:

> Nous trouverons que l'établissement de la loi et du Droit de propriété fut son premier terme; l'institution de la Magistrature le second; que le troisième et dernier fut le changement du pouvoir légitime en pouvoir arbitraire.[14]

It is as if we look through a lens, which offers us a widening field of corruption. Rousseau's arithmetic is that, the more complicated the social relations become, the greater the inequality. From rich versus poor we come to the distinction between master and slave and in the end there is only one master and also the rich become slaves. But as is so often the case, Rousseau's prose runs away with his argument. The second *Discours* is of course an indictment of the French monarchy,

[14] J.J. Rousseau, *Discours sur l'Inégalité, O.C.*, vol. 3, p. 187.

but Rousseau makes no attempt to prove that the French king is a despot. In fact later on in *Du Contrat Social*, he argues that in a large state as France rule by one man is perhaps the best solution. And what is the significance of inequality in civil society?

In the second *Discours* he makes the distinction between physical and political inequality.[15] Physical inequality means the distinction between the young and the old, the weak and the strong, and people with and without talents. Nothing can be done about physical inequality, but political inequality occurs because we use our gifts in the wrong way. Is Rousseau in favour of an equality of property and equal rights? By no means, or rather he was not interested in this question. He was proud of being a citizen of Geneva and in his *du Contrat Social* he develops a powerful concept of popular sovereignty. So the people are sovereign, but who are the people? Only those who are citizens. Rousseau completely ignored the great number of inhabitants in Geneva who had no rights at all.

In his third discourse on economic policy, which he wrote for the *Encyclopédie*, Rousseau for the first time used the term *volonté générale*.[16] Economic policy should serve the general will, because the "volonté générale est aussi toujours la plus juste, et que la voix du peuple est en effet la voix de Dieu".[17] That is well put, but what should that policy be? Rousseau mentions as a specific point that the system of taxation in France is unfair, and he is right. But the point gets lost in his general condemnation of society. He writes:

> Les hommes inégalement distribués sur le territoire, et entassés dans un lieu tandis que les autres se dépeuplent; les arts d'agrément et de pure industrie favorisés au dépens des métiers utiles et pénibles; l'agriculture sacrifiée au commerce; le publicain rendu nécessaire par la mauvaise administration des deniers de l'état; enfin la vénalité poussée à tel excès, que la considération se compte avec les pistoles, et que les vertus mêmes se vendent à prix d'argent: telles sont les causes les plus sensibles de l'opulence et de la misère, de l'intérêt particulier substitué à l'intérêt public, de la haine mutu-

[15] J.J. Rousseau, *Discours sur l'Inégalité*, *O.C.*, vol. 3, p. 131.

[16] He probably borrowed it from Diderot.

[17] J.J. Rousseau,, *Discours sur l'Économie Politique, O.C*, vol. 3, p. 246.

> elle des citoyens, de leur indifférence pour la cause commune, de la corruption du peuple, et de l'affoiblissement de tous les resort du gouvernement.[18]

Here at least he is explicit in his condemnation of the Ancien Régime, but where is his solution for the ills of France? The Physiocrats had elaborate plans for the reform of the tax system. Key to it was the plan to raise the level of productivity in the agrarian sector. And Rousseau? What does it mean that agriculture is sacrificed to commerce? What he probably had in mind was a general standstill of the economy. So that the government could sort out all the problems before it decided how to go forward. That in no sense could be a practical solution. Rousseau was a dreamer and, what is more, when he became specific he turned out to be a traditionalist. Evidently he was comparing the Roman Republic at its best as the model for his home town.

3. Du Contrat Social and Émile ou l'Éducation

Take the famous sentence of *du Contrat social*: "L'Homme est né libre, et par-tout il est dans les fers"[19]; or the one at the beginning of *Émile*: "Tout est bien, sortant des mains de l'auteur des choses: tout dégénère entres les mains de l'homme".[20] These sentences suggest that Rousseau either was a prophet of doom or a radical reformer. He was not a prophet of doom. He had some specific criticism of the tax system, but he accepted the *société des ordres* under the circumstances of which he lived.[21] In fact he profited from the protection of the Duchesse de Luxembourg and the Comtesse de Boufflers. He shared with the *philosophes* the amazing fact that he was quite content to live under the conditions of the Ancien Régime, as long of course as that regime left him in peace, which was not always the case. This first answer also applies to the question whether Rousseau was a radical reformer. Many,

---

[18] J.J. Rousseau, *Discours sur l'Économie Politique, O.C*, vol. 3, pp. 258-259.

[19] J.J. Rousseau, *O.C.*, vol. 3, pp. 354.

[20] J.J. Rousseau, *O.C.*, vol. 4, pp. 245.

[21] Diderot took care to have someone else write a lemma on political economy for the *Encyclopédie* as well.

since the nineteenth century, have regarded Rousseau as a radical. His formulation of the idea of popular sovereignty and of the general will may suggest that he was a radical democrat, but he was not.

The *volonté générale* is not a majority vote (that is the *volonté de tous*) and the general will is sovereign, which means that it cannot be delegated.

> La Souveraineté ne peut être réprésentée, par la même raison qu'elle ne peut être aliénée; elle consiste essenciellement dans la volonté générale et la volonté ne se réprésente point ... Les députés du peuple ne sont donc ni ne peuvent être ses réprésentans, ils ne sont que ses commissaires; ils ne peuvent rien conclurre définitivement.[22]

Deputies cannot be representatives; that means that they have no mandate as in a modern parliament, where the members have the discretion to vote, because a parliament in session is the sovereign body. Now this is a bizarre statement, for it means that popular sovereignty can never function in a large state such as the French monarchy. Rousseau draws this conclusion himself:

> Mais s'il est difficile qu'un grand État soit bien gouverné, il l'est beaucoup plus qu'íl soit bien gouverné par un seul homme, et chacun sait ce qu'il arrive quand le roi se donne des substituts.[23]

This quotation shows that Rousseau had no notion of practical politics. Surely a personal government by the French king existed on paper, but Louis XV and XVI did not have the power or the will to lead. Both kings had very able ministers, but as soon as they wanted to make necessary reforms they were dismissed. This happened to Turgot, when he tried to liberate the grain trade.

So popular sovereignty, in Rousseau's conception of the French monarchy (as in all large states), remains dormant. Rousseau's conclusion has to do with his definition of the *volonté générale*. The general

---

[22] J.J. Rousseau, *Du Contrat Social, O.C.*, vol. 3, pp. 429-430.

[23] J.J. Rousseau, *Du Contrat Social, O.C.*, vol. 3, pp. 410.

will is not the expression of a system of 'one man one vote', but tells us what is best for the people.

Jefferson wrote to a friend in 1816:

> The introduction of this new principle of representative democracy has rendered useless almost everything written before on the structure of government.[24]

This was not an idle boast. Representation was of course an age old principle, but the idea to couple it to a system of democratic voting was new. It was ideal for representation in a large republic such as the United States.

But could popular sovereignty only function in a democracy? Rousseau had a preference for a direct democracy, where citizens quarrelled till they reached a sensible solution for the problem in hand. That point of view harks back to the Athenian democracy or the Roman Republic during certain stages of its existence. And as we have seen it ignores the position of the so-called *natifs*, that is those who had lived in Geneva for a long time without civil rights, and pays no attention to recent immigrants. But there is more. From his *Lettres Écrites de la Montagne*, in which Rousseau took the side of those who had civil rights against the Magistrate, it becomes clear that he had a preference for an enlightened aristocracy that could govern as long as it respects the constitutional rights of its citizens. That is a conventional opinion. All eighteenth-century writers on politics, whatever their different points of view, agreed that a government should have the discretion to deal with the daily business of government without interference from a representative body.

Given how popular sovereignty could or rather could not work in practice, Rousseau's problem then became how a grown up person could lead a decent life in a not ideal situation. This was the problem he tried to solve in his *Émile ou l'Éducation.*

Rousseau makes the distinction between an *éducation domestique* and an *éducation publique.* This means that Émile first must be taught

[24] G. Brown, *The Creation of the American republic, 1776-1787* (New York 1972: Norton), p. 565.

to find his own identity before he can be trained to become a responsible citizen. This is a kind of Baptist procedure. Émile must become a moral person first before he can accept the social contract, which makes him a citizen.

Émile is twelve years old, when his education starts in earnest. He comes to live in the exclusive company of his teacher and governor. And the first thing he must learn is to make the distinction between his *amour de soi* (the notion of his true worth) and his *amour propre* (his egoism, which makes him claim things at the expense of others). This means that his peaceful soul must conquer his passion to create a world for himself, to acquire power, wealth and a reputation. Sensibility is the source of all our actions and this sensibility can easily corrupt our true understanding, as Rousseau later writes.[25] So it is essential that our sensibility works together with our reason to create the proper man and citizen.

Then Émile has been educated. He has learnt the business of cabinet making. His bride Sophie also received a special education to prepare her for the role of mother and housekeeper, but before they marry Émile undertakes his grand tour in order to decide with which country he will conclude his social contract. Then the two well-educated adults marry and decide to live in the French countryside. And they lived happily after?

By no means. In the sequel *Émile et Sophie* the couple decides, against the better judgment of each, to move to the city. Sophie commits adultery and expects a child from another man. Émile leaves his family and refuses to see Sophie anymore. In a heartrending passage, which only Rousseau could write, Sophie tries to visit Émile in his workshop. She and her little son peer through the window of his workshop, but he continues to ignore them. Years later we find Émile as a slave in North Africa. He has lost his identity as a free citizen.

What an extraordinary story. I have often wondered why Rousseau was so much admired by pedagogues in the nineteenth century. What is the point of educating a child in complete isolation? Is that not

[25] J.J. Rousseau, *Rousseau Juge de Jean-Jacques, O.C.*, vol. 1, p. 809.

asking for trouble? And why on earth did Rousseau write his sequel? To prove that the city is a wicked place, which will corrupt even the best educated adults? There are simpler means to prove this point. Why did Rousseau's schoolmaster make the extreme effort to educate a child during six years, choose a bride for him, specially prepared for the task; then make Émile decide to select the country of his choice (he could have chosen a country without wicked cities such as Paris) and then make him lose everything by a single incident? Why does he ignore Sophie who evidently is in distress when she visits his workshop? Is this not an expression of *amour propre* rather than of *amour de soi*?

The point of all these questions is that Rousseau did not write a manual on how to educate a child. What goes wrong in their relationship is that Émile loses his *amour de soi* and becomes nobody. The point of Rousseau's political writings is that only when people can lead a simple life can they become citizens and associate with others in an honest and proper way. In eighteenth-century France it is impossible for any person to guard his *amour de soi* or self-esteem and lead a decent life.

4. Rousseau among the Philosophes

Rousseau was not only a critic of the Ancien Régime but of the *philosophes* and of their efforts to reform it as well. Yet they had many ideas in common and - as we have seen in an earlier essay-[26] in religion he became the spokesman of all those who believed in a humanistic interpretation of it. To measure his position among the *philosophes* let us return to the three concepts in which Mauzi summed up how eighteenth-century writers experienced happiness.

The first is a sense of balance. It is clear that Rousseau had a different idea of balance compared to that of the *philosophes.* They wanted to introduce a sense of balance within the culture and the institutions of the Ancien Régime. Rousseau wanted to find it in a primitive past. The Enlightenment for the *philosophes* was a program of fulfilment.

[26] See the essay *Deism, Prospect or Threat.*

Reforms should improve the conditions of the Ancien Régime and, as history indicated, the advance of civilisation gave sufficient hope that these reforms could be successful. Rousseau wanted to get back and history demonstrated that things were getting seriously out of joint. On the other hand Rousseau never criticised the regime directly and he accepted the *fait accompli* that he had to live according to its conditions. In this respect he was one of the *philosophes.*

Secondly, Mauzi mentions a vivid sense of sensibility. Rousseau bewitched his contemporaries by the eloquent way in which he gave expression to this sensibility. The secret of his influence on his contemporaries is his eloquence and it gave his writings a seismographic function. Ambivalence is Mauzi's third concept. The glitter of the Court and the sociability of the *salons* could not disguise the fact that many things in eighteenth-century France went wrong. That could create a feeling of unhappiness, which Rousseau's eloquent accusations exploited. Yet on the whole the *philosophes* were rather complacent when they reviewed the ills of France, and it helped that Rousseau was not specific in his critique of the Ancien Régime. He protested several times that he was not a revolutionary. He wrote in his *Confessions* that he had always respected the government "sous lequel j'avois à vivre sans jamais désobéir à ses loix".[27]

5. The Reception of Rousseau's Ideas in the Nineteenth Century

The range of Rousseau's influence in the nineteenth-century is impressive. His influence ranges from the Romantic poets to the social reformers. Talmon is right of course, when he criticises Rousseau's idea of democracy. The appeal to direct democracy has become a fig leaf allowing despotic elites to manipulate and oppress the masses as the example of the Soviet Union demonstrates. The name suggests that the major political decisions were taken at the base, in the Soviets, but we know better. We cannot accuse Rousseau of course of having been a fellow traveller, but he inspired social reformers to accept social solutions with a certain degree of naivety. Even such hard

[27] J.J. Rousseau, "Confessions", *O.C.*, vol. 1, p. 405.

headed scientific socialists as Marx and Engels were susceptible to it. Engels' famous saying that the socialist revolution means a jump from the realm of necessity to the realm of freedom is naïve propaganda. It is not, or at least it has not been possible so far to organize a productive machinery without friction and problems, which then leaves you time to go out fishing. The Industrial Revolution is a highly unstable system, which forces us to make constant repairs to the social and economic order. There is no way that you can organize a system that controls economic growth and the avalanche of innovation. Unless you are prepared to give up innovation as the force behind economic growth.

If I have to single out a work which explains Rousseau's influence on nineteenth-century writers, it must be his *Confessions*. It is a completely honest account of his personality. Rousseau reveals himself as a hypersensitive individualist who is exclusively concerned with the impact of the outside world on his soul. That kind of individualism appealed to all those who felt the impact of an ever changing world that consequently was getting more complicated all the time. Rousseau appealed to nineteenth-century reformers and revolutionaries, because he helped them to promote their schemes as an act of faith, with often disastrous consequences for the committed and the uncommitted.

6. Montesquieu and Hume on the Balance of Powers

1. Introduction

Montesquieu did not argue for a separation but for a balance of powers. Hume believed in a separation of powers hoping in this way to reach balance in the social order. Both writers took the *status quo* within their respective countries for granted in developing their political theories. Monarchy in their opinion was the most efficient government in large countries such as France and Britain. Hume taught that monarchy (meaning an absolutist monarchy, not a limited monarchy as in Britain) was a stable form of government, and was concerned that parliament, particularly the House of Commons, would usurp the executive powers of the monarch and so create chaos. Montesquieu feared that the monarchy would degenerate into a despotic regime.

2. *Science and the Decline of Magic*

By a slow but inexorable process the belief in ghosts, witches and magic receded into the background and became folklore.[1] The scientific approach to the study of the world was responsible for this decline, but it was not the only cause or rather it was connected with the changing attitude of the professional and intellectual élite that came to mistrust any irrational explanation of events. Religion suffered because of this decline. Its magically inspired practices (such as transubstantiation) came under attack because science could prove that they did not work. Moreover, these practices could not provide any substance for the conclusions of religion's metaphysical theology.

[1] See K. Thomas, *Religion and the Decline of Magic. Studies in Popular Beliefs in Sixteenth and Seventeenth- Century England* (London 1971: Weidenfeld and Nicolson).

Yet such was the power of the new approach that many clergymen were actively involved in the 'study of man'. Hume wrote about it in the *Introduction* to his *Treatise*:

> There is no question of importance, whose decision is not compriz'd in the science of man; and there is none, which can be decided with any certainty, before we become acquainted with that science. In pretending therefore to explain the principles of human nature, we in effect propose a compleat system of the sciences, built on a foundation almost entirely new, and the only one upon which they can stand with any security.[2]

George Turnbull, chaplain to the Prince of Wales, put in the same kind of claim for the study of man in his *Principles of Moral Philosophy* (1740) and regarded it as medicine for the mind.[3] So the support for this science of man in Britain was widespread. As far as politics is concerned, Hume's ambition is manifest in the title of the essay "That politics May Be Reduced to a Science". It introduces a series of essays dealing with the politics of Hanoverian Britain at mid-century.

Montesquieu expresses his scientific approach with the lapidary sentence at the beginning of his *De l'Esprit des Lois*

> Les lois, dans la signification la plus étendue, sont les rapports nécessaires qui dérivent de la nature des choses: et, dans ce sens, tous les êtres ont leurs lois; la Divinité a ses lois; le monde matériel a ses lois; les intelligences supérieures à l'homme ont leurs lois; les bêtes ont leurs lois; l'homme a ses lois.[4]

And Montesquieu sets it down as his task to study the laws of men and their necessary connections.

I have chosen to report on the political thinking of Hume and Montesquieu because their approach to politics is in certain basic as-

---

[2] D. Hume, *A Treatise of Human Nature* (Oxford 1976:Clarendon Press), P.H. Nidditch ed., "Introduction", xvi.

[3] D. Spadafora, *The Idea of Progress in Eighteenth-Century Britain* (New Haven 1990: Yale University Press), 146.

[4] Montesquieu, *De l'Esprit des Lois, Oeuvres Complètes* (L'Intégrale, Paris 1964: Ed. du Seuil), 530.

Montesquieu

pects representative for the way politics was conceived in the world of the Enlightenment. Political thinkers in the seventeenth century focused on the problems of sovereignty and the legitimacy of authority; their eighteenth-century counterparts turned their attention to the functioning of civil society. The basic question became how individuals can work together to further not only their own interests but also those of others.

If we accept Aron's verdict that Montesquieu was one of the first sociologists, this means that Montesquieu thought in terms of collectivities.[5] The leading principle of his book is that a group is motivated by an *esprit général*, which puts an imprint on their lives.[6] Not

[5] R. Aron, *Les Étapes de la Pensée Sociologique, Montesquieu, Comte, Marx, Tocqueville, Durkheim, Pareto, Weber*, (Paris 1967: Gallimard).

[6] To use *l'esprit général* as a term for the culture of groups and nations was common usage with a Classical origin. What was new is that Montesquieu ana-

only mankind, but every group has its own laws, which apply to their members. Hume criticized this approach. He wrote in a note to his *Enquiry Concerning the Principles of Morals*:

> This illustrious writer, however set out with a different theory [in contrast with Hume's version of utilitarianism], and supposes all right to be founded on certain *rapports* or relations, which is a system, that, in my opinion, never will be reconciled with true philosophy.[7]

Hume did not protest against an approach which starts with the study of relations between men. Relations are all important in Hume's epistemology in which the relations between things perceived and things experienced gradually acquire the character of a moral universe. However Hume deals with relations between individuals, not collectivities, at least to start with. In modern jargon we should call him a 'methodological individualist', which makes him a forerunner of modern economics.

This difference of approach is visible in their political philosophy. Both were concerned with the functioning of civil society. For Montesquieu this meant the balancing act between groups to guarantee the social order. Liberty is first of all security, as Montesquieu writes:

> La liberté politique dans un citoyen est cette tranquillité d'esprit qui provient de l'opinion que chacun a de sa sûreté.[8]

Montesquieu, it is clear, is thinking of the rule of law and its effects on the safety of the citizens. Hume's conception of liberty is markedly different. Liberty is the freedom to do as one likes and the fact that civil society was a powerhouse created a political problem for Hume. Individuals try to better their lives, principally by acquiring wealth. Authority is a static fabric and must be able to withstand the dynamism connected with civil society. Politics for Hume is the effort

lyzed the factors involved in the formation of such an *esprit général*.

[7] D. Hume, *An Enquiry Concerning the Principles of Morals* (Oxford 2006: Clarendon Press), T.L. Beauchamp ed., 22, n.12.

[8] Montesquieu, *De l'Esprit des Lois*, XI, 6, p. 586.

David Hume

to maintain the balance between the dynamics of civil society and the social order, which the Magistrate has to maintain.

3. *Montesquieu's* Pouvoirs Intermédiaires *and the English Constitution*

In a study which, in my estimation, has received too little attention, Jean Jacques Granpré Molière explains how Montesquieu came to experience the English constitution during his stay in England (1729-1733).[9] Back home he wrote a piece called *La Liberté Politique* (which remained a manuscript) in which he explained that the political system in England preserved the liberty of citizens, because one political power stopped the other. In his *De l'Esprit des Lois* the famous chapter 6 in book 11 on the English constitution became an

[9] J.J. Granpré Molière, *La Théorie de la Constitution Anglaise chez Montesquieu* (Leiden 1972: Presse Universitaire de Leyde).

example in a more general theory, when Montesquieu launched his theory of the three types of government. In a republic or a democracy (for Montesquieu the terms are interchangeable[10]) virtue is the main requirement for the functioning of the republic, honour is the leading principle of a monarchy and a despotic regime maintains itself by fear. This new – more general – theory meant that Montesquieu had shed his republicanism by the time he was writing his *De l'Esprit des Lois* and became a qualified supporter of the French monarchy. Many eighteenth-century French noblemen, as A.A.M. Kinniging has shown, were republicans.[11] Reading Cicero's *De Officiis* they felt they had a duty to serve their country and they were frustrated, because they could not play an independent role in the French monarchy. Montesquieu considered that the nobility could play this role in the parliaments of France and become a *pouvoir intermédiaire* that could block any abuse of power by the monarch.[12] It is easy to understand why Montesquieu as president of the parliament of Bordeaux thought of the parliaments as such an intermediate power, but he applied his idea within his theory of the three forms of government. He explained how it could be applied in a republic or mixed forms of government and it was the object of his chapter on the English constitution to explain how this worked in Britain.[13]

There is a persistent, but erroneous idea that Montesquieu invented the doctrine of the *trias politica* or the separation of the executive, legislative and judicial powers. Even the great Montesquieu scholar Robert Shackleton cannot take leave of the idea that the separation of powers for Montesquieu was an important item. He writes:

---

[10] The idea that democracy is a regime based on the principle of one man one vote is new. Read Hume: democracy is a regime based on representation, as in the case of the Roman Republic.

[11] A.A.M. Kinniging, *Aristocracy, Antiquity and History. An Essay on Classicism in Political Thought* (Leiden 1994: dissertation).

[12] Montesquieu probably also had in mind the provincial estates, which functioned in certain parts of France and which gave representation to the third estate of privileged citizens. The national Estates General had not convened since 1614.

[13] J.J. Granpré Molière, *La Théorie de la Constitution Anglaise*, 325.

> He argues instead [against the idea that the English constitution brings together monarchical, aristocratic and democratic elements] for the mutual independence of the legislative power (entrusted to both Houses of Parliament[14]), the executive power (in the hands of the monarch) and the judicial power; and since it is only in passing that he deals with the judicial power, his contention is essentially that the legislative and executive branches of government must be in separate hands.[15]

Yet even the separation of the legislative and the executive powers is not what Montesquieu was driving at. His own idea is framed in the following sentence:

> Ces trois puissances devraient former un repos ou une inaction. Mais comme, par le mouvement nécessaire des choses, elles sont contraintes d'aller, elles seront forcées d'aller de concert.[16]

So the intermediate powers of Commons and Peers can block policy emanating from the monarch and if he or they want to get anything done they must work together. Montesquieu was thinking in terms of powers with their specific privileges and statutes. The doctrine of the separation of powers did not fit this situation. That doctrine was for the first time put into practice in the creation of the American Republic where all citizens have the same rights. As John Adams remarked, the greatest innovation of the American constitution was that "there are different orders of *offices*, but none of *men*."[17]

Montesquieu treated contemporary problems within the French monarchy with extraordinary discretion in his *De l'Esprit des Lois*. When he wanted to criticise the method of taxation in France, he referred his readers to practices in Ancient Rome and his chapter on

---

[14] And the King.

[15] R. Shackleton, *Montesquieu* (Oxford 1970: Oxford University Press), 299.

[16] Montesquieu, *De l'Esprit de Lois*, p. 589.

[17] J. Adams, *A Defence of the Constitutions of Government of the United States* (1797) (Aalen 1979: Scientia Verlag), 1: 93, cited in F.L. van Holthoon, "The Disappointment of John Adams", *Federalism, Citizenship and Collective Identities in U.S.History*, C.A.van Minnen & S.Hilton eds (Amsterdam 2000: V.U. University Press), 46.

the English constitution served the same purpose. He did not wish to introduce a balance of power English style, let alone a separation of powers into France. His point was that the French nobility must be able to play an active role as intermediate power between King and people. He was hoping against his better judgment that they could play this role, but his political analysis is in the end a form of wishful thinking. The powers in France did not work together. Royal power was ineffective and there was no alternative to its existence.

And Hume? I know of no evidence that he ever directly reacted to Montesquieu's chapter on the English constitution, but we will see that he cannot have been charmed by the idea of this intermingling of powers.

4. *Hume on the Division of Power*

Hume wrote that the *Political Discourses*, a set of essays he published in 1752, settled his reputation as a writer and philosopher. These essays were mostly on economic subjects. From 1741 Hume had published essays on the structure of the British government that came into existence since the revolution of 1688. The essay "That Politics may be Reduced to a Science" functions as an introduction to the other relevant essays.

In that essay he produces the following maxim:

> It may therefore be pronounced as an universal axiom in politics, *That an hereditary prince, a nobility without vassals, and a people voting by their representatives, form the best* MONARCHY, ARISTOCRACY, and DEMOCRACY.[18]

This is at first sight an odd axiom, because it cannot be applied to the British political system, but that is Hume's intention. His negative conclusion is that the British political system is not the best, which means to stay in a stable regime. Hume draws this conclusion in another essay, "Of the Independency of Parliament". He writes:

---

[18] D. Hume, "That Politics May Be Reduced to a Science", *Essays, Moral, Political and Literary* (Indianapolis 1987: Liberty*Classics*), E.F. Miller ed., p. 18.

> But a limited monarchy admits not of any such stability; nor is it possible to assign to the crown such a determinate degree of power, as will, in every hand, form a proper counterbalance to the other parts of the constitution. This is an unavoidable disadvantage, among the many advantages, attending that species of government.[19]

The problem, according to Hume, is that the balance of power cannot depend on property. The wealth, which the House of Commons represents, would make it the major power in the state that could interfere *ad libitum* in the business of the executive as represented by the monarch. This interference would lead to chaos and eventually to absolutist government. Hume was evidently thinking of the Commonwealth under Oliver Cromwell.

So the lesson was that the House of Commons should be moderate in its demands on the royal government and present its demands to the king in a spirit of moderation. If we keep in mind how extensive the powers allotted to the royal prerogative were, two things become clear. First of all Hume was in favour of a strong executive that could maintain public order and defend the nation. In this respect the role of the monarch in a limited monarchy as Britain in Hume's view did not differ very much from that of the French king in an absolutist monarchy as Montesquieu did accept it. Secondly, Hume's idea of a separation of powers excludes the possibility of a parliamentary democracy.[20] No monarch could accept the mandate of the House of Commons as a leading principle and manage to stay in power according to him. In "Of the Origin of Government", an essay which appeared after his death, Hume gave his final assessment of the nature of this authority:

> In this sense, it must be owned [of a free government "which admits of a partition of power among several members"], that liberty is the perfection of civil society; but still authority must be

[19] D. Hume, "Of the Independency of Parliament", *Essays*, 46.

[20] In which the executive derives its mandate from parliament and the members of parliament have a mandate of the voters.

> acknowledged essential to its very existence: and in those contests, which so often take place between the one and the other, the latter may, on that account, challenge the preference.[21]

There is a trade off between authority and liberty. The House of Commons should respect the right of the monarch and his government to exercise authority, and the monarchical government should respect the right of his subjects to conduct their lives in the way they want. Hume remained vague about what that right implied. He gives us no clear definition of the fundamental rights of the citizens and so it is hard to determine when these rights will be violated. In his *Treatise* he considers the possibility of revolt against an existing government and he is parsimonious in admitting the legitimacy of this revolt:

> The common rule requires submission; and 'tis only in cases of grievous tyranny and oppression, that the exception can take place.[22]

Were the actions of James II a case of grievous tyranny? In describing the revolution of 1688-1689 in his *History of England*,[23] Hume was not so sure that the revolution was justifiable. At the same time, from early on in his writing career he was convinced that people make revolution because they want, not because they have a right to do so.

There is another reason for leaving civil society to its own devices. In this way civil society can prosper and create the vitality and fun for doing things. Hume writes:

> In times when industry and the arts flourish, men are kept in perpetual occupation, and enjoy, as their reward, the occupation itself, as well as those pleasures which are the fruit of their labour.[24]

---

[21] D. Hume, "Of the Origin of Government", 41.

[22] D. Hume, *A Treatise*, III, 2, x, 554.

[23] D. Hume, *A History of England* (Indianapolis 1983: Liberty*Classics*), chapters 70 and 71.

[24] D. Hume, "Of Refinement in the Arts", *Essays*, 270; arts stand here for artisan and commercial occupations.

Take away the possibility for these activities and indolence and fatigue will be present. This was Hume's image of civil society and the most remarkable aspect of it is that people do not only generate wealth in pursuing their activities, but also have fun and add to the mental health of society.

So Hume's assessment of the situation, which the revolution of 1688 and its settlement had created, was that it had brought into being a situation which should be handled with care. On the one hand the limited monarchy, which was the result of the revolution, was unstable. On the other hand it was the only regime suitable to guarantee the dynamism of civil society. His recipe was to keep the executive and the legislative powers separate as much as possible.[25] Hume's ideal was an efficient but limited executive that held a close watch on the requirements of an expanding economy.

By contrast Montesquieu held a static view of society.[26] His concern was how the balance of the existing powers in the French kingdom could guarantee the rule of law. Hume agreed that the administration "must act by general and equal laws".[27] Both the executive and the legislative have the duty to maintain and obey these laws, but Hume had to make way for the dynamism of civil society and hence he advocated his version of the separation of powers.

4. *Political Theory and the Enlightenment*

Leslie Stephen wrote in 1876:

> During the quieter hours of the eighteenth century Englishmen rather played with political theories than seriously discuss them.[28]

[25] As Montesquieu already remarked, no one talked about an independent judicial power. The situation of that power was too complicated to talk about its independency.

[26] His *De l'Esprit des Lois* contains many comments on French history, but they nowhere lead to an analysis of the regime of Louis XV.

[27] D. Hume, "Of the Origin of Government", *Essays*, 41.

[28] L. Stephen, *History of English Thought in the Eighteenth Century* (New York 1881: Forgotten Books fac. ed. 2012), vol. 2, 131.

Leslie Stephen

That remark not only applies to Englishmen, but also to Frenchmen and other Europeans. There was a general feeling that the existing regimes might need some tinkering with, but on the whole they met national specifications for stability. Rousseau was of course the obvious exception, but Hume and Montesquieu were not. Their ideas represented the political thought of the Enlightenment on two counts. In the first place they both looked for a policy of moderation, which could correspond with balanced human relations. Secondly, Montesquieu accepted the *status quo* of the political structure for his long ranging discussions, and Hume went so far as to defend it as the only possible recipe for political stability. I have called this a recipe to implement the end of history, by which I mean that it is the only way to ensure political stability in the future.

The idea of the end of history does not put an end to the progression of events through time but, assuming that the right measures are taken, these events will not contain the surprises of unintended effects, which will threaten stability. It is hard to imagine how the French elite thought that the Ancien Régime could survive without drastic reforms. Only a few individuals – Turgot, Gournay and the Physiocrats – saw this need, but they stood no chance against all the interests invested in the Ancien Régime. Perhaps the most surprising aspect of political thought in the French Enlightenment is that when the Estates General convened in May 1789 no one had a clear idea what the alternative to the Ancien Régime should be, except Sieyès who published his famous pamphlet *Qu'est-ce que le Tiers État* in January of that year. That proclaimed that the third estate was the nation. However, he had no idea what that nation was and how it was supposed to function.

Part of an answer to the mystery why the established classes accepted the *status quo* with equanimity is that the Enlightenment primarily promoted a cultural program of improvement.[29] The *philosophes* wanted to civilize and to educate, not to undertake political reforms. Yet it remains odd that no one saw the storm of the French Revolution coming.

Hume faced a different situation in Britain. The economy was a going concern, but could it be left to its own devices? In most of his economic essays he was optimistic and even complacent in his conclusion that economic activities would lead to social harmony and increasing wealth, but there is one essay in which he was not so confident. Hume and Adam Smith were determined opponents of an increasing public debt. In his essay "Of Public Credit" he writes:

> These are men, who have no connexions with the state, who can enjoy their revenue in any part of the globe in which they chuse to reside, who will naturally bury themselves in the capital or in great cities, and who will sink into the lethargy of a stupid and

[29] Some, like Montesquieu who was promoting the improvement of viniculture, were interested in reform on a personal basis, and we should not forget the impact of these personal efforts. How else would we drink chateau-wines today?

Turgot

> pampered luxury, without spirit, ambition, or enjoyment. Adieu to all ideas of nobility, gentry, and family.[30]

What could the collusion of the royal government with the financiers mean? First of all the royal government by borrowing could bypass parliament, which controlled the expenditure of government. That would destroy the balance of power between parliament and monarch. However the evil influence of the financiers went much further. Corruption could disrupt the existing ties of loyalty and duty within civil society, and government by going on borrowing would destroy itself.

The passage quoted from Hume's "Of Public Credit" has a prophetic quality. The great transformation, which occurred after Hume's death in 1776, which we call the Industrial Revolution, has certainly

[30] D. Hume, "Of Public Credit", *Essays*, 357-358, see also "Of Civil Liberty", *Essays*, 95.

destroyed the ties of loyalty and duty as Hume experienced them. Today not only public but also private debts are threatening to disrupt the global economy. If it is true that the cash nexus determines human relations, they do not seem to make for stable relations.

VII. Economics and the Science of Administration

1. Introduction

John Stuart Mill's *Principles of Political Economy* of 1848 became Alfred Marshall's *Principles of Economics* in 1890. The change of title marks the development of economics into an autonomous field of inquiry. Economists since 1890 could (and would) give advice to politicians about how to administer the economy, but they concentrated their attention on the study of economic relations. That is not how the study of economics started its career. Sébastien de Vauban's *Projet d'une Dixme Royale* (1707) dealt with tax reform and William Petty's *Political Arithmetic* (published 1690) provided the statistics needed by the administration. For the French Physiocrats and the German Cameralists, fifty years later, the reform of the administration was their main concern. Of course they also saw it as their objective to promote prosperity, but even so they argued as administrators. More prosperity meant a greater yield of taxes.

In Britain the perspective was different. There was no need for fundamental economic reforms. Economic forces lead to reform by itself and cleared away obnoxious regulations such as those associated with the guilds. The main message of economists such as Adam Smith and David Hume was to promote the free trade of goods where possible. However, those economists were not doctrinaire advocates of a *laissez faire* policy. Smith, for instance, accepted the navigation acts (so hated by the Dutch), because they were needed for the defense of the nation.[1] Both Hume and Smith were aware that their observations on economic life in Britain had to fit social and political realities.

[1] A. Smith, *An Inquiry into the Nature and Causes of the Wealth of Nations* (Oxford 1976: Clarendon Press), R.H. Campbell & A.S. Skinner eds, vol. 2, pp.

There is one further general remark to be made before I turn to the specifics of eighteenth-century economic science. Economists of that age are primarily interested in flow or an optimal circulation of goods and not in growth. This becomes clear from Gournay's slogan *laissez faire, laissez passer*. Gournay was an important official in Louis XV's government and his focus was on the elimination of domestic tolls, cumbersome excises and obnoxious custom duties. The notion of the economic circle as developed by Richard Cantillon and François Quesnay served the same objective. Let the flow of goods and services, from production to consumption, take its natural course and so add to prosperity. That is also the message of Adam Smith's *Wealth of Nations*. The moment that economic growth turned into a policy-objective came much later.

In what follows I will take my examples from Germany, Austria, France and Britain, to corroborate the general perspective in all these countries, but at the same time to highlight the major differences between Britain and the continent in the way they exploited opportunities.

2. *The Prussia of Frederick the Great*

Frederick II (reign 1740-1786), is regarded as the prime example of an enlightened despot. Enlightened he was in the sense that he took a lively interest in the French Enlightenment; he wrote in French and preferred French in conversation with his courtiers. In his *Anti-Machiavel*, which he wrote just before he became king, he announced himself as the first servant of the state and indeed he worked hard as king to fulfill this role.

He was enlightened, because he was in favour of religious toleration and to a certain extent allowed everybody to think for himself, but he ordered them to act as he wished. In the confrontation between the *philosophe* (so Frederick preferred to regard himself) and the despot, the latter won out.

464-465. They did not oppose impressments for the same reason. Hume called it a "remarkable custom".

Adam Smith

Frederick was a despot with an iron fist. He had a special reason for behaving like this. He earned his epithet 'great', because he almost single handed put Prussia on the map as a major European power. His policy of expansion was not on the agenda of the Enlightenment. The abbé de St. Pierre published a plan for arbitration between the European princes, and Voltaire, though skeptical about the feasibility of such a plan, preferred peaceful cooperation between nations to war and expansionist policies. In this view he was joined by most of the philosophers of the Enlightenment.

Frederick's plans for reform were geared to his dream of creating a greater Prussia. Prussia had the highest literacy rate in Europe, because Frederick needed well-trained soldiers. Freeing the peasants from feudal burdens was also part of his plans for reform, but in this case

Frederick did not get very far, because he not only needed soldiers, but also officers, and those the Prussian *Junkers* had to provide. So he had to have a regard for their wishes and interests and this made the liberation of the peasants a long winded process that stretched out to the middle of the nineteenth century. Frederick left as a troublesome legacy the militarization of Prussian life, which would haunt Prussia and Germany till the defeat of Germany in 1945 and the disappearance of Prussia from the map of Europe.

The greatest achievement of his reign was the codification of *das allgemeine Landrecht.* Ernst Ferdinand Klein, a loyal and conservative jurist who helped to create this new code of laws wrote:

> Man hat, meiner Meinung nach, nicht wohl getan, dass man den Grossen das Selbstherrschen gar zu sehr angepriesen hat. Die berühmtesten Selbstherrscher waren nicht immer die vorzüglichsten Regenten.[2]

And so the Prussian king became the victim of his own reforms, because the new code made it impossible that the king could turn the course of justice to his own advantage.

3. *The Habsburg Empire*

Maria Theresa and her sons, the Emperor Joseph II and Leopold II, were the Austrian counterparts of Frederick the Great. Maria Theresa had a kind heart, but she was a bigot who relentlessly persecuted Jews and Protestants in her empire. However, she and her sons realized that they had to modernize the bureaucracy and create a uniform law system in their ragbag of principalities. Joseph von Sonnenfels and Johann von Justi, civil servants of the Empire, were dedicated *Aufklärer* who wanted to educate and uplift the people, free them from feudal burdens and promote industry. The yield of their efforts was mixed. The *robot* (a system of forced labour) was abolished and so serfs legally became peasants. However, according to the new regulations, the peasant had to work three days in the week for his lord, but "the

[2] Cited in I. Mittenzwei, *Friedrich II von Preussen. Eine Biographie* (Keulen 1980: Pahl-Rugenstein), 194.

empress and the coregent [later Joseph II] found it difficult to enforce even the three days outer limit".[3]

In the nineteenth century the Austrian-Hungarian Empire had an efficient bureaucracy. Yet the reforms had come and were coming from above and left little room for democratization until it was too late.

4. *The Physiocrats in France*

Joseph Schumpeter's *History of Economic Analysis* is the bible of that history. The book combines erudition and a mastery of technical details. Schumpeter has a preference for Richard Cantillon's *Essai sur la Nature du Commerce en Général (1755)* and Turgot's *Réflexions sur la Formation et la Distribution des Richesses (1769),* compared to Quesnay's *Tableau Économique* (1758) and to Adam Smith's *Wealth of Nations* (1776). Schumpeter writes about Turgot:

> Such as it is, ..., Turgot's theoretical skeleton is, even irrespective of its priority, distinctly superior to the theoretical skeleton of the *Wealth of Nations.*

And:

> It is not too much to say that analytic economics took a century to get where it could have got in twelve years after the publication of Turgot's treatise had its content been properly understood and absorbed by an alert profession.[4]

Schumpeter has a preference for those economists who are able to raise economic transactions to a level of abstraction where they become variables in a web of interacting causes. He has a problem with Quesnay and Adam Smith because they start their analysis with one variable - with Quesnay that is the *produit net* and with Smith it is the quantity of labour – which then more or less monitors the other variables in the economy. Quesnay and Smith are first of all

---

[3] R.A. Kann, *A History of the Habsburg Empire, 1526-1918* (Berkeley 1977: University of California Press), 197.

[4] J. Schumpeter, *A History of Economic Analysis*, 248-249.

interested in the practical problems of their own time and that focus determines their approach to economics, and that is why they single out the factor which to them is of the greatest importance. That is also the reason why their thought should take pride of place in this essay.

Before I turn to Quesnay's *Tableau Économique* I must mention Jean Claude Maria Vincent de Gournay first. He is an elusive figure in the history of economic thought. Schumpeter praises him "as may have been one of the greatest teachers of economics that ever lived".[5] However, we know very little about Gournay's ideas, because he never published anything. He taught Turgot and promoted Cantillon's work and, as an influential civil servant, he spent his life in trying to reform the French economy. He came from a family of merchants and knew that liberty of trade was more important than its regulation.

Quesnay was the physician of the French king and his mistress Mme de Pompadour.[6] As such he lived in an entresol of the palace at Versailles. There he invited his friends and started the physiocratic movement. His followers included the Marquis de Mirabeau (father of the revolutionary whom he had locked up as a young man to teach him a lesson) and Dupont de Nemours, who emigrated during the French Revolution to the United States, where he founded the chemical works, which still bear his name. Quesnay's major ideas are the *produit net*, the *impôt unique* and the circular flow of the economy. The *produit net* is the simple idea that a farmer sows his grain and harvests his crop. Yield minus seed corn is the *produit net.* The not so simple idea attached to this is that *only* the farmers produce wealth, which then circulates through the economy.

The French tax system had the effect that the burden of taxes oppressed the peasants. Oppressed peasants are bad producers and Quesnay wanted to reform the system so that producers could see the point of improving their methods of farming. Quesnay's solution was

---

[5] J. Schumpeter, i*bidem.*

[6] His medical expertise may have come in easy. His idea of the scheme of economic circulation was probably inspired by Harvey's discovery of the circulation of blood, which was regarded as one of the great discoveries of the seventeenth century.

to tax the landowners. In his circular system the *produit net* came into the hands of the landowning class. This was the time to reserve part of it for administrative purposes before the landowners distributed the *produit net*: this logic Quesnay exemplified by his scheme of the circular flow of the economy in his *Tableau Économique.*

Quesnay distinguishes three classes, the productive class, which produces the *produit net*, the distributive class that distributes the *produit net* by buying food and finished wares from farmers and artisans. These artisans form the sterile class, because they refashion raw materials, but add no value to them. Obviously there also is an exchange between the productive and the sterile classes. The productive class needs goods, the sterile class food. The spending of the distributive class also has the effect that the sterile class can afford to buy food from the productive class. When the circle is completed the productive class has again produced a new *produit net* that it delivers to the distributive class. So we get the following scheme:

```
DISTRIBUTIVE CLASS
▲                                  ▲
| |                                | |

| |                                | |
▲                                  ▲

PROD. CLASS--------------------->
                       STER. CLASS
          <------------------------
```

In a detailed tabulation Ronald Meek introduces complicating factors such as foreign trade and investments in capital goods and he shows how even with these complications the circle turns round and in due time the *produit net* is delivered to the distributive class for a

Joseph A. Schumpeter

new round of distribution. I hope I have said enough to discuss the following characteristics of the scheme.[7]

1. Quesnay's most controversial concepts are the *produit net* and the sterile class of artisans and traders. Sterile does not mean that the artisans are not productive, but the term indicates that their production depends on the productivity of the farmers. Agricultural productivity is the directive force in the economy. And so the concept of *produit net* perfectly suited the reform plans of the Physiocrats. Create the condition for a better productivity of the farmers and the society as a whole and the state will profit.

As an analysis of the French economic situation anno 1750, Quesnay's *Tableau Économique* made sense, but as a general economic statement it is defective. It is similar to the advice of walking on one

[7] R.L. Meek, *The Economics of Physiocracy* (London 1963: Allen & Unwin), pp. 284-286.

leg. It is possible but uncomfortable. Furthermore it did not fit the situation in Britain. So we can understand that Adam Smith criticised the concept.

2. Meek's tabulation pays attention to the investment in capital goods. The main investors are supposed to be the farmers. They should be farmers and entrepreneurs and for this role Quesnay was looking to the *fermiers* in Northern France. They were keen on using modern techniques and equipment in exploiting their soil and Quesnay hoped that as part of his reform they would replace the unproductive peasants in the whole of France. Quesnay admired the situation in Britain in which the nobility played an active role in the agricultural economy, but apparently he thought that the French nobility was not fit for this role.

3. Quesnay did not allow for savings in his system other then needed for investment in equipment, buildings and goods. There had to be an easy and uninterrupted flow of money on its circular route and he warned for *épargnes stériles*. You could regard him as a precursor of John Maynard Keynes, but it seems more the case that the abstract nature of his scheme did not allow for the distinction between useful and harmful savings (if you want to make the distinction).[8]

The plans for reform came to nothing. Turgot, who favoured the idea of the *impôt unique* and who had learned from Gournay how important it was to introduce a free trade of corn, became *contrôleur général des finances* (minister of finance and public works) in 1774, and introduced it. It was a bad moment, the seventies had a series of bad harvests and grain prices rose steeply. The clamour of the people rather than the will of the king led to Turgot's dismissal. Would Turgot have been able to prevent the French Revolution? Perhaps, but that was not because of his advocacy of free trade. As Schumpeter writes:

[8] Quesnay also frowned on a too sumptuous consumption by the nobility, because that could effect their buying of food from the farmers and hence diminish the *produit net.* But how could he prevent such 'irresponsible' behaviour, when he did not assign any active role for the nobility in the economy?

> If we mean the overthrow of the monarchy and the sanguinary excesses, the answer should be in the affirmative: no more, however, because of the reforms he might have carried in that case, than because of his willingness to call out the troops. No cap of liberty will fit Turgot.[9]

Indeed the general weakness of the royal government that did not believe in its own authority was a major cause of the Revolution. Sensible reforms did not stand a ghost of a chance under the regime of Louis XVI. We may also ask whether reforms which took the Ancien Régime for granted could be successful. The ease with which the social structure came tumbling down after 1789 suggests that the institutions of the Ancien Régime could not provide a basis for reforms.

5. *Hume, Adam Smith and the Agrarian Revolution*

Since the seventeenth century the so-called 'agrarian revolution' led to a spectacular increase of output in crops and livestock. This revolution was caused by a number of factors. The enclosures since medieval times cleared away the small holdings of the open field villages and made it possible to introduce new methods of cultivation. New ploughs, seed drills and the cultivation of lupines and clover produced fodder for the cows and crop rotation made it unnecessary to leave fields fallow every third year. Improvement in agriculture was also the result of the cooperation between tenants and landlords. Among these latter were noblemen with vast estates, who invested in drainage, farm building and the infrastructure, and farmers who invested in new agricultural techniques. It is clear that the landlords preferred capitalist farmers (to use David Ricardo's term) to poor peasants. These peasants lost their independence and became farm labourers.

While the term 'agrarian revolution' was of a later date, eighteenth-century propagandists for agricultural reform, such as Arthur Young, promoted reform with great enthusiasm. However, they did not consider what took place in the countryside as a revolution. That term came into use when it was linked to the industrial revolution. Frie-

[9] J. Schumpeter, *History of Economic Analysis*, p. 247.

drich Engels was one of the first who used it in 1834 and afterwards commentators became aware that something extraordinary new was happening. Subsequently the term agrarian revolution was coined. In the eighteenth century, however, the new developments in industry and agriculture could still be fitted in a familiar world that was not likely to change very much and people could not conceive that it would alter out of recognition. This fact we should keep in mind when I discuss the economic thought of Hume and Adam Smith.[10]

A great number of competent economists appeared in eighteenth-century Britain, but I want to show how economists took the existing social order for granted, working on the analysis of the economic system. And as Hume and Adam Smith are regarded as creative economists and representative for the ideas of the Enlightenment, they are ideal for pointing out that on the one side they were enthusiastic about new developments and on the other side did not expect that these developments would corrode and eventually destroy the existing social order.[11]

I already cited Hume's remark that industrial activities not only produce wealth, but that they invigorate the society and create pleasure. That remark comes from an essay entitled "Of the Refinement of the Arts". Its original title was "Of Luxury" and in it Hume took issue with the conventional idea that luxury would lead to moral decay. Luxury adds to the comfort of life and the refinement of sensibilities. And that was the reason Hume changed the title of his essay.

Writers since Montesquieu took the view that economic activity would lead to peaceful and civilised manners.[12] Hume belongs to

---

[10] Another Scottish economist of note was Sir James Steuart, who made a plea for the development of the Scottish economy and for this goal was in favour of intervention by the government. See his *Inquiry into the Principles of Political Economy* (1767) (Edinburgh 1966: Oliver & Boyd), where A.S. Skinner provides a biography in his introduction.

[11] I reported in a former essay that Hume had a premonition of this possibility.

[12] A.O. Hirschmann, *The Passions and the Interest, Political Arguments for Capitalism before its Triumph* (Princeton 1977: Princeton University Press).

this group of writers. For him economic activities do not mean that what I take you lose. All participants can profit from the cooperation between economic actors. Cooperation is an essential element of economic transactions. While the Physiocrats emphasized the national aspect of this cooperation, Hume emphasized the international aspects of it:

> Thus *industry, knowledge,* and *humanity,* are linked together by an indissoluble chain, and are found, from experience as well as reason, to be peculiar to the more polished, and, what are commonly denominated, the more luxurious ages.[13]

Hume and Adam Smith were no liberals in the sense that economic liberty was their first priority. They accepted the regulation of trade for reasons of state and we have seen that Smith accepted the Navigation Act. On the whole they regarded them as sensible, because national defence is more important than wealth.

Well-known of course is Adam Smith's metaphor of the invisible hand:

> By preferring the support of domestick to that of foreign industry, he intends only his own security; and by directing that industry in such a manner as its produce may be of the greatest value, he intends only his own gain, and he is in this, as in many other cases, led by an invisible hand to promote an end which was no part of his jntention.[14]

This quotation is remarkable for two reasons. First Smith was aware (like many of his contemporaries) of the importance of unintended effects. The sum total of human activities is a blind process, which nobody can control. And, secondly, Smith was convinced that this blind process would lead to equilibrium. Donald Winch has

[13] D. Hume, "Of the Refinement in the Arts", *Essays,* 271.

[14] A. Smith, *Wealth of Nations,* vol. 2, p. 456. Smith was very proud of this metaphor. He used it twice more, in his *Theory of Moral Sentiments* and in his *History of Astronomy.* Smith was the first economist who employed a model to explain economic relations and was aware that the model influenced what he saw. He was much more intelligent than Schumpeter takes him for.

warned us not to study Smith from a liberal capitalist perspective.[15] Equilibrium and the unobstructed flow of goods were more important to Smith than economic growth. Smith starts his chapter 2 with his famous definition of the division of labour. This division is not the outcome of human foresight, but of the "very slow and gradual consequence of a certain propensity to truck, barter and exchange one thing for another".[16] This is not propaganda for economic liberalism in a nineteenth-century sense. Smith wants to point out how a natural economic order can come into existence, when people cooperate by pursuing their own interests.

In his analysis Smith explains that wages, profits and rent are the component parts of the cost price of a finished product. Labourers earn wages, which means that they are living more or less at the subsistence level. Profit is the recompense of the capitalist who saves and invests. His capital is in effect hoarded labour and so he saves first and then invests. Credit should serve first of all the purpose of facilitating the flow of capital, and it was considered risky to give it for the reason of future expectations. Rent is the recompense for the landlord's property of land and though Smith is not very clear on this point, he probably regards it as the only monopoly value which is acceptable. The quantity of labour controls the values of the component parts. Schumpeter is critical about this theory of value and calls it a detour from real insight in the economic process, which ends with Ricardo, Mill and Marx. However, in Smith's world, to make the quantity of labour the measure of value makes sense, because, while the labourer is living at the subsistence level food prices determine the productivity of the economy. In this respect he was as much a Physiocrat as the Physiocrats themselves, but he adds a new twist to the story based on his experience with the British experience:

[15] D. Winch, *Adam Smith's Politics. An Essay in Historiographic Revision* (Cambridge 1978: Cambridge University Press).

[16] A. Smith, *The Wealth of Nations*, vol. 1, 1, 2, & 1, p. 25.

> The capital error of this system [of the Physiocrats], however, seems to lie in its representing the class of artificers, manufacturers and merchants, as altogether barren and unproductive.[17]

His reasoning is simple. If the merchant does not carry grain to the market and so adds value to it, the grain will rot in the fields for the greater part. Smith's criticism – though the term 'capital error' is harsh – does not demolish the Physiocratic scheme but enlarges it. It adds trade and industry to it as independent factors.[18]

Smith's vision of the role of economics in society comes out clearly in his chapter 4 in Book III, "Of the Principle of the Commercial and Colonial Trade." In it he offers a sharp and critical account of the monopolies and subsidies in the colonial trade:

> The monopoly of the colony trade, therefore, so far as it has turned towards that trade a greater proportion of the capital of Great Britain than what would otherwise have gone to it, has in all cases turned it, from a foreign trade of consumption with the neighbouring, into one with a more distant country; in many cases, from a direct foreign trade of consumption, into a roundabout one; and in some cases, from all foreign trade of consumption, into a carrying trade.[19]

So the colonial trade disrupts the natural flow of capital based on the symbiosis of agriculture, trade and industry. The irony of Smith's advocacy is that the Scot who has the reputation of introducing free trade as a slogan in nineteenth-century politics regarded it as a weapon against the merchants, particularly the colonial merchants who tended to outwit other classes in society, the landlords in the first place. And just as Hume, Smith looked askance on those internationally oriented capitalists who threatened the happy symbiosis. He re-

---

[17] A. Smith, *Wealth of Nations*, vol. 2, 4, & 9, p. 674.

[18] If we can catch Smith walking on one leg it is because of his distinction between productive labour, which adds value to the economy, and unproductive labour that does not. Civil servants and schoolteachers are in the latter category. And their example shows that the distinction cannot be made, for of course they add value to the economy, even if only indirectly.

[19] A. Smith, *Wealth of Nations*, vol. 2, p. 607.

garded the existing social order of labourers, capitalists and landlords, as the guarantee for an economic equilibrium, which was the product of citizens who were active in pursuing their own interests without hurting the interest of others.

6. *Enlightened Political Economy*

Reform on the continent meant reform of the rural economy. Efforts in this direction were not spectacularly successful. In Britain the idea was that the civil society could take care of economic progress and according to Smith and Hume, only monopolies, which distorted trade, had to be eliminated.

The general notion of enlightened political economy was to create an equilibrium based on the cooperation of all economic agents. Of course the increase of national wealth was a desirable goal, but the main objective was to allow for the optimum flow of goods and capital. Flow might produce more wealth, but flow not wealth was the priority to which economic thought was directed.

The central weakness of this vision of economics was that it paid to little attention to the position of the peasants in the land and the labourers in the towns. They had no political rights, very often they had the status of displaced persons who were only registered in criminal records, if at all. And it was regarded as a normal fact of life that they lived on the subsistence level. It was the great challenge of the nineteenth-century to include them in the social and political order.

VIII. The Black Side of the Mirror: Love, Lust and the Marquis of Sade

1. *Introduction*

Suzanne Curchod, a protestant girl from Lausanne, was the love of Gibbon's life. His father forbade him to marry her and Gibbon, better in the role of sympathetic uncle than as lover, complied. Suzanne became a remarkable woman. She married the banker Necker and as Mme Necker she was Gibbon's *confidante.* He was not the only one. She lent her sympathetic ear to a number of famous men. So she sat at the bedside of the dying Buffon. In retrospect Gibbon wrote about his love for her:

> I understand by this passion the union of desire, friendship and tenderness, which is inflamed by a single female, which prefers her to the rest of her sex, and which seeks her possession as the supreme or the sole happiness of our being.[1]

This quotation could serve as a motto for a longer study about experiencing love in the eighteenth century. Such a study cannot be undertaken here, but something must be said about it to justify the title of this essay.

It is extremely difficult to know how our ancestors experienced love. We have the classical literature on famous love affairs of course, but did they mirror everyday life? The official rules about what was permitted in sexual relations were clear. Only married couples are allowed to have sex, and not so much for pleasure as for the duty of procreation. We know at least that in the *salons* of the French Enlightenment no one took these rules seriously. They functioned as a shield behind which everyone made his own choices. Many opted

[1] *The Autobiography of Edward Gibbon* (London 1923: Dent), D. Smeaton ed., 78.

for the aristocratic solution. One married to secure offspring and the continuity of the family line. After marriage the man (and often his wife) sought a new partner in love. The sober minded Montesquieu was married (curiously enough) to a protestant lady. Love was not an issue in their partnership. She managed his affairs and he had a mistress in a village nearby *La Brède*, his castle. Of course this breach of conjugal fidelity could be an invitation to promiscuity – *libertinage* as it was called – but purer souls saw a love affair as a means of separating business and emotional involvement. Love for the philosophers of the Enlightenment was an opportunity to discover the possibilities and constraints of human nature. They regarded love as the human motive that could promote agreeable relations between human beings. I have been struck by the love affair of Voltaire and Mme du Châtelet.[2] Voltaire moved in with her at Cirey, her seat in provincial France. Her husband, the Marquis, was also present in this *marriage à trois* and apparently he did not mind Voltaire's presence. Later, when love had petered out, Voltaire remained her loyal friend. He was at her bedside, when she was dying expecting a baby from St Lambert, the poet. Voltaire could turn love into friendship and he showed a degree of sophistication, which regrettably is lacking in many modern couples.

Love for Gibbon was an emotional investment in the unique other person. The French noblemen were notoriously unfaithful to their wives and the British nobility will not have behaved very differently, I suspect. However, the British bourgeoisie more and more made it their objective to invest this emotionally in marriage. We have no conclusive evidence for this statement nor do we know how their behaviour compared with that of the French bourgeoisie. In his *Centuries of Childhood* Philippe Ariès makes the point that the well-to-do bourgeoisie started to focus on the privacy of their domestic lives and began to pay particular attention to the education of their children and –of course– in the first place their sons.[3] A professional education became at least as

[2] Immortalized in Nancy Mitford's *Voltaire in Love.*

[3] French dissertation 1960, English version (Harmondsworth 1973: Penguin); see also F.L. van Holthoon, *Mensen in Europa, Ontwerp voor een Sociale Geschiedenis van Europa* (Alphen a.d. Rijn 1977: Samsom), 121.

important as the cultivation of manners. This is an extremely interesting thesis though Ariès does not really manage to substantiate it in historical terms. The same is true for Edward Shorter's *The Making of the Modern Family*. He argues that romantic love was an essential element of the modern family. Again his argument that the bourgeois marriage, as inspired by romantic love, was an innovation which turned marriage into a very successful and much discussed nineteenth-century institution, is important and probably true.[4] However, I remain dubious about his historical evidence.

So the motto derived from Gibbon raises an important point and not only because the emotional investment in love tells us something about the modern family. The philosophers of the Enlightenment regarded love as a tonic for the health of human transactions.

In what follows I will discuss novels of Samuel Richardson and Choderlos de Laclos. Laclos, the writer of *Les Liaisons Dangereuses*, wrote to his wife from Italy in 1801:

> Le motif de l'ouvrage est de rendre populaire cette vérité qu'il n'existe de bonheur que dans la famille.[5]

Les Liaisons Dangereuses was Laclos' first and only novel. At the time he wrote to his wife he was thinking of writing a sequel, presumably, on marital bliss. Even writing his first novel Laclos was influenced by *Pamela* and *Clarissa*, two novels by Richardson. His novel was about the dangers of *libertinage*, but at the back of his mind was a concept of marriage in which man and wife married for love. He almost certainly wanted to celebrate a new type of marriage – bourgeois marriage – in his new novel.

And Sade? For him love did not exist and marriage was an obsolete institution. A call for cooperation was hypocritical for *homo homini lupus*. His idea of man and society contrasted sharply with that of the *philosophes*. Hence the title of this essay.

---

[4] (Glasgow 1977: Fontana).

[5] J. Grape, *Les Liaisons Dangereuses de Choderlos de Laclos* (Paris 1997: Gallimard).

Laclos and Sade were both influenced by *Pamela* and *Clarissa.* They developed the themes of Richardson in opposite directions. Laclos focussed on the necessity of love in human relations and Sade was particularly intrigued by the rake Lord Lovelace. The contrast, which in this manner emerges, can help us to understand Sade's intellectual world and his historical significance.

2. *Defining Marital Bliss, Richardson's* Pamela *and* Clarissa

A novel of course is no sociological report on human conduct. It betrays the preferences of the author on how people should or should not behave. Richardson's message in this respect is clear. At the end of 1500 pages of fine print (in my edition) he writes that *Clarissa* answers to the "religious plan" of God's providence.[6] This providence sees to it that virtue will be rewarded as with Clarissa and sin will be punished as in the case of Lord Lovelace who raped Clarissa. Lovelace is killed in a duel: "This wilful transgressor [is] condignly punished"(1498) and which truthful Christian will not envy "Clarissa's triumphant death"?[7]

> Whose piety from her early childhood, whose diffusive charity; whose steady virtue; whose Christian humility; whose forgiving spirit; whose meekness; whose resignation, HEAVEN, only could reward? (1498).

This is Richardson's conventional message, but he has another one, which is more interesting and which makes it worthwhile to discuss his novels in this essay.

Richardson published *Pamela* in 1740 and 1741. The subtitle indicates his second message: *Pamela or Virtue Rewarded.* What is the reward? Pamela is a lady's maid who was inherited by a nobleman at the death of his mother. She is a beauty with a modest background and she is harassed and intimidated by her 'master' who has taken a fancy

---

[6] S. Richardson, *Clarissa or the History of a Young Lady*, 1747/1748, (London 1985: Penguin), A. Ross, after the edition of 1798.

[7] Richardson makes no attempt to explain why she had to die. I suspect her death suited his moral purpose.

Samuel Richardson

to her and wants to make her his concubine. Defending her virtue like a lioness she beseeches him to send her home to her parents. He imprisons her instead in one of his country seats, but she remains adamant in her desire to return home. Eventually he gives in and agrees to send her home. He does so in a letter in which he declares his love for her and that letter changes everything. Pamela writes her parents:

> O my dear parents forgive me! but I found, to my grief before, that my heart was too partial in favour; but *now*, to find him capable of so much openness, so much affection, nay, and of so much *honour* too, I am quite overcome (283).

So the master and his maid marry and Pamela becomes the mistress of the house to the consternation of his family and friends. That sudden switch from intimidation to a declaration of love on the one hand and from frantic resistance to the acceptance of his love is a bit artificial, even though she confesses that she had some feelings for him. Cynically one might say that her steadfast resistance brought her a good party. However, this is not what Richardson meant by reward. He only writes about love between the two when they are married, and suggests that the proper channel of love is marriage; and Richardson's message has a sequel. In her "high condition" (386) she lists an impressive list of charities, which she plans to undertake. Furthermore she formulates 48 rules for treating her husband. The last rule gives her *quid pro quo* for obeying her husband at all times:

> That a husband, who expects all this, is to be incapable of returning insult for condescension; and ought not to abridge her of any privilege of her sex (480).

Clearly she is the dynamic force that reforms her husband's life and she introduces the norms of a bourgeois style of living in his noble family.

The tragic story of *Clarissa* is that she first is the victim of the greed of her family that wants her to marry a man she loathes. Lord Lovelace helps her to escape from home, but he has the sinister plan to seduce her. So he lodges her in a (rather posh) brothel (it takes her a long time to find out where she is). Lord Lovelace is a rake who rapes her after she has been drugged, because he cannot reach his objective in another way. The unravelling of the plot is that Clarissa pines away till she dies and Lovelace discovers to his horror that he genuinely loves her and that he has gambled away his chance to be loved. In a moment of truth he writes to his friend Belford:

> "Shall I give thee a faint picture of the horrible uneasiness with which my mind struggles? And faint indeed it must be; for nothing but outrageous madness can exceed it, and *that* only in the apprehension of others; since, as to the sufferer, it is certain that actual distraction (take it out of its lucid intervals) must be an infinitely more happy state than the suspense and anxieties that bring it on.
>
> Forbidden to attend the dear creature, yet longing to see her, I would give the world to be admitted once more to her beloved presence (1333-1334)".

Clarissa only pities him with the damning words: "Poor man, said she! I once could have loved him." (1341).

This then is the story of unfulfilled love. *Pamela* has a happy ending and *Clarissa* is a tragedy, but the message in both novels is the same. Love between man and woman is a case for mutual esteem and can only prosper in the married state.

3. *Richardson's Reception in France*

Richardson's novels were well received in France. Diderot wrote an *Éloge de Richardson* and was impressed by Richardson's treatment of semblance and reality. History is full of lies, Diderot wrote, and Richardson's novels are full of truths.

> Le cœur, qui a été, est et sera toujours le même, est le modèle d'après lequel tu copies ... Sous ce point de vue, j'oserai dire que souvent l'histoire est un mauvais roman ; et que le roman, comme tu l'as fait, est une bonne histoire. O peintre de la nature! C'est toi qui ne mens jamais.[8]

Semblance equals the hypocrisy of human relations. The French aristocracy could indulge in *libertinages* as long as the semblance of the conventional moral code remained unimpaired, but true love unmasks this hypocrisy. In his *Éloge* Diderot is not acting the moralist, but being a student of human nature he concludes that true love is the dynamic principle of history. He is not thinking of the social effects of love in the first place, but of what insight true love affords us into the character of human nature. Clarissa for Diderot is a heroine, because her honesty and purity shows her rapist in the true light of a perverted soul.

Laclos' only novel immediately became a classic (though Gustave Lanson only mentions it in a note in his authoritative *Histoire de la Littérature Française*). Who regards lovemaking as a game and mis-

---

[8] D. Diderot, *Oeuvres Complètes* (Paris 1875-1877: Garnier), J. Assérat & M. Tourneux eds, 39-40; quoted in R. Goldberg, *Sex and Enlightenment. Women in Richardson and Diderot* (Cambridge 1984: Cambridge University Press), 143.

takes pleasure for happiness is bound to be disappointed and will feel empty and bored in the end.

Laclos was an artillery officer in the royal army and he had only to look around him to notice the antics of the society in which he moved. He himself lived a happy bourgeois life with his wife and children. He had a brilliant inventive mind, but his achievements were not noticed in the army during the Ancien Régime or the Revolution. He played an important role during the victory of the revolutionary army at Valmy, but it was Carnot, not he, who earned the reputation of being the saviour of the French nation. Under Napoleon he served as one of his generals. While on duty in Italy he died near Taranto in 1803. He earned his reputation of being the author of a saucy novel by mistake. In no way is his book pornography. No bawdy word came from his pen. He gave a cool and precise analysis of sexual relations in the upper class circles of the Ancien Régime, and to accentuate his objective approach he used the model of the epistolary novel. Laclos wrote about what had happened, not about what did happen.[9] That gives his commentary on events a reflective air. The epistolary model was common in his time. Richardson used it, so did Rousseau., but Laclos used it in a masterly fashion. Every correspondent is given his or her own style of expression. He also had a fine sense for the paradoxes imbedded in human relations and that also determined his craftsmanship. René Pomeau wrote a study called *Laclos ou le Paradoxe.* [10] In what follows I will use his interpretation of *Les Liaisons Dangereuses.*

The Count of Valmont and the Marchioness of Merteuil, two ex-lovers, plan a scheme (*projet* in Laclos' military terminology) to seduce Céline de Volanges, introduce her to the lifestyle of *libertinage* and prepare her for marriage to the count of Gercoult. That project succeeds. Valmont seduces Céline and she learns the pleasures of *libertinage* and to feign love. The second project is much more difficult. Valmont must also seduce Mme de Tourvel, the young wife of an

---

[9] For this reason alone Roger Vadim's film made after the book has an entirely different format.

[10] (Paris 1993: Hachette).

Chodlerlos de Laclos

elderly president of the parliament at Paris. Her virtuous and pious behaviour is an obvious obstacle. Valmont writes to Mme de Merteuil that for him it is not enough to force himself on Mme la Présidente "et d'en faire une nouvelle Clarisse". "Ce n'est pas assez pour moi de la posséder, je veux qu'elle se livre."[11]

Eventually he succeeds in his mission and then things go horribly wrong. Mme de Tourvel believes she has found the love of her life, but soon discovers that she has been tricked. She finds refuge in a nunnery, where she languishes away in true Clarissa-fashion. While she is dying Valmont becomes desperate. He beseeches Mme de Volanges (the mother of Céline) to deliver his letter to the mortally sick woman. I have put a knife in her heart, but I am the only one who can pull it out and save her, he writes. Laclos omitted the letter from the

[11] Choderlos de Laclos, *Les Liaisons Dangereuses* (Paris 1995, Garnier). Y. LeHir ed., 259.

printed version of his novel. Instead he suggests that Valmont discovers that he loves Mme de Tourvel, but as in the case of Lovelace that realization comes too late and he also dies in a duel.

Mme de Merteuil, the other principal character in the novel, is an impressive woman, notwithstanding her depraved manners. She pays back her lovers in kind. She describes to Valmont how she got married and participated in "le tourbillon du monde".[12] Then she becomes a widow and decides never to marry again. She loves her independent status and her motto becomes "que l'amour qu'on nous vante comme la cause de nos plaisirs, n'en est plus que le prétexte."(177). I have acquired a reputation of being unapproachable and that façade allows me to choose my lovers on my conditions. Her luck also runs out. When her intrigues become common knowledge the audience jeers at her when she visits the Opera. At that moment small pox has covered her with black spots and she has become a monster. She, however, accepts her fate with stoic resignation. Laclos depicts her as a strong woman until the end. Earlier I cited Laclos' letter to his wife that happiness can only be found in the family. The main objective of Laclos is to point out the risks of *libertinage*, but in the way he pays homage to Richardson it becomes clear that true love goes together with fidelity and affection, and those were the main ingredients of the bourgeois marriage. So Laclos -himself a nobleman at the lowest level, an *écuyer*– became the propagandist of the modern family.

4. *The Biography of the Marquis de Sade*

Sade spent most of his adult life in prison or a lunatic asylum. It was his mother in law who had him locked up by royal decree, the so-called *letter de cachet.* This stamped letter made it possible to lock up people without due process, simply because they were considered obnoxious. Sade was kept in the fortress of Vincennes, then in the Bastille, and he had the bad luck of being transferred to the asylum of Charenton, days before the Bastille was stormed by the crowd, on July 14, 1789. Shortly afterwards he enjoyed a short period of

[12] Letter 81.

Marquis De Sade

freedom till again he landed, this time, in a revolutionary prison. He escaped execution, because the revolutionaries forgot to bring him before the tribunal the day before Robespierre was executed and the period of Terror ceased. When he was again put away Charenton in deed became an asylum for him, because he could no longer take care of himself. Royer-Collard, a civil servant, wrote to the chief of police under Napoleon, Fouché, that Sade was not mad but utterly depraved and that he had to be transferred to an ordinary prison (fortunately for Sade, this did not happen).[13] Sade, indeed, was not mad; being a nuisance was reason enough to lock him up under the Ancien Régime. Mirabeau, the famous revolutionary tribune, spent time in the Bastille, when Sade was also an inmate. The son of the writer of

[13] M. Foucault, *History of Madness* (London 2006: Routledge), J. Khalfos ed. & J. Murphy trans., 107.

L'Ami du Peuple was an inveterate gambler, and his father hoped to cure him by *lettre de cachet.*

We owe to Sade's imprisonment a great number of curious novels and plays, among them *Les 120 Journées de Sodome, ou l'École du Libertinage*, which may be regarded as Sade's philosophic textbook. He wrote this voluminous work in a month's time at night. He glued the sheets together and turned the manuscript in a scroll, which he kept carefully concealed in his cell. After the fall of the Bastille, Sade lost all his books and personal belongings, when the mob vandalized the fortress, but his scroll remained undetected. Somewhat later a member of the staff discovered it and the manuscript stayed in a family archive till it was sold at the beginning of the twentieth century. It was almost immediately published and helped to fortify Sade's reputation as a writer and philosopher.

The editor of the English translation dedicated his edition to Maurice Heine, who greatly contributed to Sade's rehabilitation, with the words: "To the memory of Maurice Heine, who freed Sade from the prison wherein he was held captive for over a century after his death."[14] Sade has had many critics who defended his works in recent times. Amongst them , curiously enough, a number of women. Sade, after all, regarded women as objects.

I must confess I have little sympathy for the man and consider him a dull philosopher, but whether Sade was nice or a deep thinker is not the point. Imagination, Sade wrote, is a powerful aphrodisiac. It is one of his better statements. The imagination is the strongest impulse to the generation of ideas. In Sade's case this impulse had a sinister tendency, but it is to this tendency that Sade owes his importance as a writer.

5. *The Philosophy of the Bedroom and the 120 Days of Sodom*

Sade left an impressive written legacy, but his philosophy is repetitive, and the two works I have chosen for further discussion are representative for the lot. In his *Philosophie dans le Boudoir* (boudoir is strangely

[14] Marquis de Sade, *The One Hundred & Twenty Days of Sodom*, London 1991:Arrow Books), A. Wainhouse & R. Seaver eds, vi.

translated as bedroom??) the young girl Eugénie is initiated in the delights of *libertinage*. In the process she loses all sense of shame and she is trained in all the practices dear to Sade. Part of the initiation is of course that she loses her virginity, but ordinary sex is not the point of Sade's *libertinage*. Sade had a preference for anal sex, masturbation, and so on. And then of course we have coprophily. The word was new to me. My edition of the *Oxford Concise Dictionary* mentions coprofagous as the habit of dung eating beetles. Eating the excrement of your partners in lust seems to create a paroxysm of sexual excitement.

Actions in the lady's boudoir are coupled with commentary on man and society. The Chevalier de Mirval gives a long discourse on the free republic (the novel was published in 1794 during the Revolution). Freedom means that there are no limits to pursuing your own ends. Parents are not responsible for their children –let them be raised in special institutions– nor are children for their parents. Love does not exist, only lust does and so we must have brothels for men as well as women. In the Chevalier's republic men as well as women must unconditionally submit to the cravings of members of the other (or the same) sex.

Crime is not important nor is calumny, and what in fact is profanity? Theft is a method of taking from the rich, and murder to further your sexual pleasures is a necessity rather than a crime. Cruelty, the infliction of pain, must be accepted as a natural form of behaviour.

After the philosophical discourses the partners bring the philosophy into practice. The mother of Eugénie, who comes to save her child, is raped by a servant infected with syphilis and to prevent the poisonous seed leaving her body, Eugénie, now an accomplished libertine, sews the vagina of her mother. The mother is led away by the Chevalier and the rest of the party stays behind in rapture.

If after reading this we recover from the first shock, it is time to ask what we should think of this extraordinary set of events. Our sexual mores have become more tolerant, but cruelty and murder? Simone de Beauvoir writes about Sade:

> His chief interest for us lies not in his aberrations, but in the manner in which he assumed responsibility for them. He made of his

> sexuality an ethic; he expressed this ethic in works of literature. It is by this deliberate act that Sade attains a real originality.[15]

Sade as the moralist of evil? That sounds as a beautiful paradox, but what has that to do with ethics? For that, as I see it, deals with the mutual benefits of those involved. Sade can only think of himself. A second conclusion of Beauvoir is more to the point:

> The supreme value of his testimony lies in its ability to disturb us. It forces us to re-examine thoroughly the basic problem which haunts our age in different forms: the true relation between man and man.[16]

Indeed Sade's writing hurts us deep in our souls. Sade was not a great thinker but the *120 Days of Sodom* has the nature of a sinister prophecy.

In the remote castle of Silling four gentlemen organize 120 days of orgies. Their retinue consists for the greater part of small boys and girls who will become the innocent victims of these perverse men. Day by day we get the elaboration of their repertoire. Sade makes it clear that these children are victims and feel themselves to be victims. A small girl is caught praying to God for her deliverance. She is in double jeopardy. Praying to God is a heinous sin, for God does not exist. And wanting to get away spoils the pleasure of the four gentlemen. She is punished, but she is not the only one. Most of the objects of lust are murdered in the end. Sodom ends in an orgy of torture and murder. Sade's laconic summing up of these tortures and murders is almost unbearable to read.

There is a gradual unfolding of the scenario. It starts (n.b.) relatively innocently and ends with the annihilation of all the flesh which has been abused. This is Sade's message: lust goes together with a craving for power over others, not to direct but destroy them. Sade is a nihilist and that nihilism points uncomfortably at modern tyrants, such as Hitler, Stalin and Pol Pot. Freud, reflecting on Hitler's emergence to power in Germany, wrote about *eros* and *thanatos.* Eros

15 S. de Beauvoir, "Must we Burn Sade?", Sade, *The 120 Days of Sodom*, 6.

16 S. de Beauvoir, "Must we burn Sade?", 64.

means love and approaching others; thanatos is the lust to destroy all that is within the power to destroy as victims.

6. *The Dark Side of the Mirror*

Hume writes:

> In general we may remark, that the minds of men are mirrors to one another, not only because they reflect each others emotions, but also because those rays of passions, sentiments and opinions may be often reverberated, and may decay away by insensibly degrees.[17]

His point is that, analysing our own feelings, we learn to recognize them as being akin to those of others and he uses the metaphor of the mirror to explain how we can recognize the other by analysing the self. This recognition (through sympathy, the term Hume uses) is the basis of fellow feeling and cooperation, and those two terms were of crucial importance for the philosophers of the Enlightenment.

Sade's arrogance, his extravagancy and sexual behaviour mark him as a representative of the Ancien Régime rather than of the Enlightenment. That regime punished him rather mildly. He was on several occasions guilty of extreme forms of sacrilege. Others received the death penalty for less.

His radical opinions have a certain relationship with those of the Enlightenment. Like Hume, he appealed to human nature to justify his philosophy. Yet there the comparison stops, for Sade is only interested in exploring *his* human relationship. Elaborating his fantasies in prison he only finds himself. Sade the egotist argues that nothing is important outside of him. Virtue is a straitjacket, applied by the established powers. As such it does not exist in nature. How different is the verdict of Voltaire, Hume and Rousseau! All three distanced themselves from the Christian definition of virtue. For them virtue is not a sacrifice, but a bonus, because it brings people together.

---

[17] D. Hume, *A Treatise of Human Nature* (Oxford: Clarendon Press, P.H. Nidditch ed.), II, 2, v, 365.

Sexuality was an important theme for the philosophers of the Enlightenment, because it made people approach each other in friendship. Love did not only serve the purpose of procreation, but it was the yeast in human relations. After his survey of libertine behaviour Laclos concluded that love is only safe within marriage. This was at the time more a British than a French opinion, but in the nineteenth century it became a main ingredient for the success of the bourgeois marriage everywhere in the Western world.

For Sade this idea of channelling sexual feeling within marriage was ridiculous. Sex can only serve perfunctory encounters in which every individual is on his own. Sade is sometimes compared to Max Stirner, the writer of *Der Einzige und sein Eigentum*, because both were solipsists in the extreme. However, from his solipsist position Stirner was prepared to negotiate with society, Sade was not. Other people remained for him other people. Sade's sinister message is that the impulse of *thanatos* is lurking in all of us and that under certain circumstances lust is an efficient way of unleashing the impulse to destroy. That message is the dark side of the mirror. If for the philosophers of the Enlightenment cooperation leads to a better and more civilised life, Sade regarded cooperation as a fiction and a ploy.

IX. The Idea of Progress and the End of History

1. *Introduction*

Of course many eighteenth-century writers believed in progress. The problem is that the idea had no repercussions. It remained the vague idea that mankind, particularly in Europe was getting more civilized. J.B. Bury wrote a long report on the quarrel between the Ancients and the Moderns and quoted Charles Perrault:

> La docte Antiquité dans toute sa durée
> Á l'égal de nos jours ne fut point éclairée.[1]

That sounds promising, but all that Perrault had in mind was freeing literature from the tyranny exercised by the humanists since the Renaissance, who dictated that the Classical models should be strictly followed. David Spadafora has pointed out that the Christian idea of linear progression remained an important source of inspiration for British authors in the eighteenth century.[2] However, amongst them the relation between progress and providence was far from clear. Bossuet wrote an eloquent story of providence in his *Histoire Universelle* of 1684, and he ended his story with the reign of Louis le Grand (Louis XIV), which was the culmination of Christian civilization. Now Bossuet had no problem explaining how mankind got to the seventeenth-century French monarchy, for the biblical story explains the route. However, the philosophers of the Enlightenment had to find the sign of progress in a secular human history, and the remarkable thing is that they did not even try. In another context Hume's argument in the *Dialogue* at the end of his *Enquiry Concerning the Prin-*

[1] J.B. Bury, *The Idea of Progress* (New York 1955: Dover), 84.

[2] D. Spadafora, *The Idea of Progress in Eighteenth-Century Britain,* 321.

ciples of Morals focussed on how, in Classical Greece, homosexuality and the murder of former friends were functional to society, because these manners were accepted. This might read as an invitation to cultural relativism, but Hume was firmly convinced that eighteenth-century Scottish morality was by far superior to Greek morality. So how did we get from Greece to Scotland? Hume had no intention of explaining this and if we repeat this question to Voltaire or William Robertson we also draw a blank.

But if eighteenth-century society was so much better than that of Greece, what about utopian schemes in this century? When we think about the Enlightenment, Carl Becker's *The Heavenly City of the Eighteenth-Century Philosophers* has accustomed us to think of it in utopian terms. However, utopias did not play an important role in the discussions between these philosophers. Abbé de St-Pierre's scheme of perpetual peace was cited by Bury as a prime example of such a utopian scheme, but the plan of the Abbé is, as we shall see, pragmatic, if not very realistic in the short term.

We might formulate the problem of this essay by remarking that the eighteenth century philosophers had an idea of progress, but no theory of it. No theory of progress? What then about the four stages theory? The four stages are 1. the stage of hunters and food gatherers, 2. the stage of the shepherds, 3. the stage of the farmers, and 4. the stage of commercial society. Ronald Meek has shown how the theory was discussed in the eighteenth-century and led to a sociology of the different stages. What is not so clear is whether those who used the theory presented a clear projection of progress in four stages, or merely presented a commentary on different ways of life.

I have argued in an essay on Hume's *History* and the End of History[3] that his set of essays on English politics makes it clear that the *regimen mixtum* that came into existence in Britain after 1689 was unstable. It could only work, when the King respected the Commons and the Commons did not interfere with the daily business of government. That recipe for stability I call the end of history, because

[3] F.L. van Holthoon, 'Hume and the End of History', *David Hume, Historical Thinker, Historical Writer*, (University Park PA: Pennsylvania State University Press), M. Spencer ed.

it leaves no option for a substantial reform of the system. It is either stability on Hume's terms, or chaos.

In France there were no outspoken statements on politics, basically because no one talked about politics or rather political science in the *salons.* As far as the *philosophes* are concerned, it means that they were critical about details of the Ancien Régime but had no attention to topple it.

Bury pays a lot of attention to Condorcet's *Esquisse.* And indeed with his *Esquisse* Condorcet provided a theory of progress. However, it is a product of the revolution and there is very little in Condorcet's career during the Ancien Régime, which prepares us for his role during the Revolution. He is an example how writers can drastically change their perspective under the influence of a shift in public opinion. There is another astonishing example of this. J.C.D. Clark carefully documents in his *The Language of Liberty* the political discourses among English dissenters.[4] This discourse led to Richard Price's reply to Edmund Burke's *Reflections on the Revolution in France* and Tom Paine's *The Rights of Man.* Price and Paine introduced a new definition of human rights, which formerly had remained *sub rosa* till the Revolution provoked people like Price and Paine who turned the discourse into a new radical message.[5]

This introduction sets down my task. I shall first of all pay attention to the peace plan of the Abbé de St Pierre. Then I shall turn to a discussion of the four stages theory, and I will deal with Voltaire, Hume, Robertson and Gibbon, to substantiate my point that all of these writers have an idea of progress but not a theory of progress. Finally, I will show that Condorcet's *Esquisse* contains a theory of progress because it adds the new element that progress is not only possible but that it will necessarily occur.

---

[4] J.C.D. Clark, *The Language of Liberty, 1660-1832. Political Discourse and Social Dynamics in the Anglo-American World* (Cambridge 1994: Cambridge University Press).

[5] They were not alone. See Jeffeson's famous second sentence in the Declaration of Independence : "We hold these truths to be self-evident, that all men are created equal, that they are endowed by their Creator with certain unalienable."

2. *The Peace-Plan of the Abbé de St-Pierre*

Voltaire called him Saint-Pierre d'Utopie,[6] but he was rather a pragmatic busybody than a utopian schemer.

Charles François Castel de Saint-Pierre (1658-1743) belonged to "la bonne, sinon à la meilleure noblesse de Normandie".[7] As a son of the aristocracy he had the choice between the army and the church as a career. He chose the latter. It was said that he was about the only abbé who kept the vow of celibacy though he was not a practicing Catholic, let alone a practicing priest.

Saint-Pierre was a man of plans. He made one for the education of girls; he designed a chair, which would ease back pain; and there was his *Projet pour Rendre la Paix Perpétuelle entre les Souverains Chrétiens*, which appeared in Utrecht in 1717. It is a boring book to read, because Saint-Pierre constantly repeats himself. He justified his repetitive style by saying that he wanted to draw attention to the important points of his project. That was a bad advice for himself and his reader who easily loses his way in the 719 pages of a modern edition. However, Saint-Pierre was no fool, as is demonstrated by the following summary of his plan.

1. All European princes conclude an alliance, which gives them security against foreign and civil wars.
2. Each prince contributes to a fund for maintaining peace.
3. A conflict between partners in the alliance will be settled by arbitration.
4. When a prince refuses to obey a decision taken by three quarters of the members he can be forced to obey.
5. New rules can be added by a unanimity of votes to the basic rule that war will never again be used to settle a conflict within the alliance.[8]

---

[6] J. Drouet, *Abbé de Saint-Pierre. L'Homme, l'Oeuvre* (Paris 1912: Honoré Champion), p. 334.

[7] J. Drouet, *Abbé de Saint-Pierre*, p. 3.

[8] Abbé de Saint-Pierre, *Projet pour Rendre la Paix Perpétuelle entre les Souverains* (Paris 1986: Fayard)123-124.

Abbé de St Pierre

This cannot be called a utopian scheme. It presages the Holy Alliance of Czar Alexander that had to be a bulwark against revolution (1815). And indeed the most remarkable aspect of Saint-Pierre's scheme is that it is an alliance of princes, not of nations. This betrays his conservative outlook. Otherwise his rule that princes can be forced to obey the fundamental rule to submit to arbitration is quite forward. It makes him the forerunner of institutions of arbitration in the present day, such as the International court in The Hague. However, there is no trace of an idea, let alone a theory of progress in his project.

3. *The Four Stages Theory*

Next to Meek, John Pocock has dealt with the theory of the four stages in the fourth volume of his *Barbarism and Religion.*[9] Meek

[9] J.G.A. Pocock, *Barbarism and Religion,* vol. 4, *Barbarians, Savages and Empires* (Cambridge 2005: Cambridge University Press).

Edmund Burke

reconstructs the story as moving through four stages leading up to the situation as we know it today. I prefer Pocock's treatment of the theory, because he stops in the eighteenth century and looks at the theory of stages as intellectuals of the eighteenth century used it to suit their situation.

Seen from this perspective the theory of stages served two purposes. First of all it could help to find an answer to the question on how we can match the biblical story with the new experience of the expanding colonial empires. The Europeans met savages for the first time in person, particularly the North American Indians, and linked their experience to the history of the Chinese, Persians and Turkish empires, and to the story of the Huns and the Islam. The second purpose, particularly evident in Voltaire's *Essai sur les Moeurs*, was to find a secular alternative to *l'histoire sacrée*, to history as the message of God's revelation to the Christians.

Goguet seems to have been one of the first who used a theory of the four stages in his *De l'Origine des Lois, des Arts et des Sciences*, which was published in 1758 in three volumes. Pocock's chapter dealing with Goguet's work is entitled "The Confusion of the Tongues and the Origin of Civility". Goguet fitted new material about Persian and Chinese empires into the biblical story starting with the building of the tower of Babel which, according to the Bible, led to the confusion of tongues. Goguet used the four stages theory to stress the importance of the stage when people settled down to become farmers. This was for Goguet the origin of civilization, leading to its culmination in the monarchy of Louis XIV. If we follow the use of the theory, apart from Goguet we first of all meet Turgot.

a. Turgot

In 1750 as student at the Sorbonne Turgot delivered a speech "Sur les Progrès Successifs de l'Esprit Humain". Turgot considered intellectual achievements to be the force of progress. There is no mention yet of the theory of the four stages. That came two years later in a sketch, which was only published in 1808. So Turgot's legacy to a theory of progress was that his assistant Condorcet picked up his notion that the progress of ideas is at the centre of a general theory of progress.

b. *Adam Smith*

In 1752 Smith became professor of moral philosophy in Glasgow. His lectures were very popular and some students made transcriptions, presumably to sell these to other students. In 1897 Edward Cannan published one of such transcription, and in 1958 a second set of notes was discovered. Together they were published as Smith's *Lectures on Jurisprudence*. In these lectures Smith must have said:

> There are four distinct states which mankind pass thro: 1st, the Age of Hunters; 2dly, the Age of Shepherds; 3dly, the Age of Agriculture; and 4thly, the Age of Commerce.[10]

[10] A. Smith, *Lectures on Jurisprudence* (Oxford 1978: Oxford University Press),R.L. Meek, D.D. Raphael and P.G. Stein eds, 14.

This is a clear statement of the theory of the four stages, but Smith only used his theory to point out how property rights came to be established moving from stages 1 to stage 4. In his *Wealth of Nations* – that is the age of commerce – he had no need for the theory.

c. *Adam Ferguson*

Ferguson's *Essay on the History of Civil Society* (1767) provides the most detailed formulation of the four stage theory. Ferguson, however, was not interested in a theory of progress. His four stage theory provides, according to Meek, an "evaluation of both the savage state and the modern commercial state".[11] Ferguson pointed out the hazards at each stage and, as far as commercial society was concerned, these hazards were the decline of military valour and the dangers of the division of labour for the workers involved.[12]

d. *John Millar*

According to John Millar:

> There is thus, in human society, a natural progress from ignorance to knowledge, and from rude to civilized manners, the several stages of which are accompanied with peculiar laws and customs.[13]

That sounds promising, but the way Millar treated the civilizational process is rather one- sided. He wrote that he used the theory:

> To mark the progress of society, with regard to the power of the husband, the father, and the civil magistrate.[14]

He demonstrated how gradually –through the stages– the position of women improved.

---

[11] R.L. Meek, *Social Science and the Ignoble Savage*, 154.

[12] Adam Smith shared Ferguson's fear that the division of labour would turn workers into mere brutes.

[13] J. Millar, *The Origin of the Distinction of Ranks* (Bristol 1990: Thoemmes), J.V. Price intr., 4.

[14] J. Millar, *The Origin of the Distinction of Ranks*, 243.

Millar's work on *The Origin and Distinction of Ranks*, though popular in his time, was, I think, inferior to the works of Ferguson and Smith. He introduced a general notion of human progress, but that seems to end in his own time. The distinction of ranks is there to stay and the idea that mankind will and must progress, which would turn his idea into a theory of progress, is absent.

The way these philosophers of the Enlightenment used the four stages theory was to enlighten the public for a special purpose, and their approach opened no vista on the general progress of mankind.

4. *Four Historians: Voltaire, Hume, Robertson and Gibbon*

If a theory of progress should be evident, it is in the histories of these four representatives of philosophical histories, but it is not there. History for Hume was no engine of progress. He wrote at the end of his history:

> Above all, a civilized nation, like the English, who have happily established the most perfect and most accurate system of liberty that was ever found compatible with government, ought to be cautious in appealing to the practice of their ancestors, or regarding the maxims of uncultivated ages as certain rules for their present conduct. An acquaintance with the ancient periods of their government is chiefly useful by instructing them to cherish their present constitution, from a comparison or contrast with the condition of those distant times. And it is also curious, by shewing them the remote, and commonly faint and disfigured originals of the most finished and most noble institutions, and by instructing them in the great mixture of accident, which commonly concurs with a small ingredient of wisdom and foresight, in erecting the complicated fabric of the most perfect government.[15]

[15] D. Hume, *A History of England* (Indianapolis 1985: Liberty*Classics*), vol. 2, p. 525. Richard Hurd said that Hume wrote his *History* as witches say their prayers: backwards. Hume started with two volumes on the Stuarts, then followed with one volume on the Tudors, and he ended his history with two volumes on medieval history. So volume two of this set was the last he wrote.

This is an advice to both the Tories and the Whigs not to trust old formulas, but concentrate on the present. That is what history teaches us. The reading of history must liberate us from the past.

a. Voltaire

Voltaire wrote a number of histories. Among them *Le Siècle de Louis XIV* and the *Essai sur les Mœurs* are the more important ones. His *Siècle de Louis XIV* came first (1751). It was a great success. He glorified the reign of the King, because his firm administration brought peace and because he made Versailles the centre of culture in France. Given Voltaire's criticisms of the rulers who came after him, this *laudatio* may be surprising, but Voltaire also had two major criticisms of Louis the Great. The eviction of the Huguenots from France in 1685 was a grave mistake. The revocation of the edict of Nantes was a direct breach with Henry IV's policy of religious toleration and, secondly, Louis' ambition to gain hegemony in Europe was illusory and brought France on the verge of ruin. How do we match the *laudatio* with this criticism? I think Voltaire wanted to point out to Louis XV (Louis XIV's grandson) how to administer France in a fair and firm way, and maintain the court as the centre of culture. Louis XV could do neither.

I did not discover the point of Voltaire's *Essai sur les Moeurs* (1756), till I read Pocock's second volume in the series *Barbarism and Religion.*[16] He made it clear to me that Voltaire wanted to create an alternative to biblical history as world history. Voltaire pointed out that the world had seen other centers of civilization beside Christianity. As an answer to Bossuet's Christian-centric version of universal history he presented a secularized version. But Voltaire's *Essai* remained Europe-centric. The Chinese and the Persian empires had had the great merit of adopting a sort of ecumenical monotheism, but Voltaire's history culminated in the institution of Christian monarchy, of which eighteenth-century France was the model.

---

[16] Vol. 2, *Narratives of Civil Government* (Cambridge 1999: Cambridge University Press).

If we consider how difficult it was to get away from the biblical story, Voltaire's *Essay* has considerable merit. Again it was a celebration of monarchy as the most advanced regime. Many contemporaries in and outside France shared Voltaire's belief that a monarchy was the most modern regime and that republics are only fit for city-states. The American Republic was founded (1787) about only forty years later. That republic turned into a successful regime and a world power.

b. *Hume*

What kind of history did Hume write? Duncan Forbes writes:

> A history of civilization ... and a political history at the same time and the two aspects of the *History* fuse – the history of civilization bares its teeth in the arena of politics in the first volume Hume published.[17]

This dental metaphor is not correct. Hume wrote no *history* of civilization. He delighted in writing extensive notes and added four appendices, but he excused them himself as digressions from his main story, which was about political history. This point needs to be made, because he had a neo-classical opinion of how to write history. According to this opinion the story must be presented as a continuous whole with a clear scenario. In his *Enquiry Concerning Human Understanding* he writes:

> And always, he [the historian] is sensible that the more unbroken the chain [of events] is, which he presents to his reader, the more perfect is his production.[18]

Hume used the conventional form of the chronicle to present his unbroken chain. Each English king has its chapter or chapters. However, behind this conventional façade Hume conceals an ambitious focus. As a Scot, he looked with fascination at the evolution of Eng-

[17] D. Hume, *The History of the Reigns of James I and Charles I* (Harmondsworth: Penguin 1970), D. Forbes, "Introduction", 39.

[18] D. Hume, *An Enquiry Concerning Human Understanding* (Oxford 2000: Clarendon Press), T.L. Beauchamp ed., 19; Hume deleted the passage in the posthumous edition 1777.

lish kingship. In English history it was the natural centre of central government: something, which was lacking in Scotland. He wrote to his printer William Strahan in 1757 that he should have started his *History* with the Tudors: "It is really the Commencement of modern History".[19] According to Hume the Tudors installed absolute kingship in England and the history of the Tudors make it clear why he considered absolute kingship a modern institution. Of course, he was also aware that fundamental economic and social changes were beginning to appear in Tudor England and in the Western world in general. However, precisely because of these changes England needed kings who could maintain their authority.

These changes were of consequence for the development of kingship since the Tudors, for the Tudor kings never managed to organize a standing army, and so they remained vulnerable to popular pressure. When Charles I went too far in the direction of the French type of absolutism, he lost his head. Hume considered the outcome of the revolution of 1688 to be a happy, but unstable one, because of the uneasy accommodation of civil liberty and (what in fact remained) absolutist kingship.

In book II, after Richard III had been slain at the battlefield of Bosworth, Hume gave a general overview of the times to come:

> Thus we have pursued the history of England through a series of many barbarous ages, till we have at last reached the dawn of civility and sciences…[20]

And Hume is fully aware of what this 'dawn' implies. A page further on he adds:

> The rise, progress, and the decline of art and science, are curious objects of contemplation, and intimately connected with a narration of civil transactions. The events of no particular period can be fully accounted for, but by considering the degrees of advancement, which men have reached in those particulars.[21]

---

[19] D. Hume, *Letters* (Oxford 1969:Clarendon Press), vol. 1, 251.

[20] D. Hume, *The History of England*, vol. 2, 518.

[21] D. Hume, The History of England, vol. 2, 519.

The way he solved this problem was by adding often copious notes to his political history, but in doing this he developed no theory of progress. Even in his political history he did not think in terms of a constitutional evolution. In a note he added to the fourth volume in 1762, he wrote that "The English constitution, like all others, has been in a state of continual fluctuation",[22] not evolution.

c. *William Robertson*

Robertson, Principal of Edinburgh University and a moderate minister in the Church of Scotland, wrote *The History of the Reign of Emperor Charles V* (1769). His preface to his history bears the promising title "A view of the progress of Society in Europe". Felix Gilbert remarks in his introduction to a separate edition of this preface that it has a providential character.[23] Robertson described the revival of civilization since the dark ages as part of the divine scheme for the future of Christianity. He ends his history with the following remark:

> It was during his administration [that of Charles V] that the powers of Europe were formed into one great political system, in which each took a station, wherein it has since remained with less variation than could have been expected after the shocks occasioned by so many internal revolutions, and so many foreign wars.[24]

That is as close Robertson gets to a general statement about the reign of Charles V. His *History* is a bland description of battles and political intrigues. Robertson describes how events led to a system of an international balance of powers and he leaves it to the reader to draw his own conclusions. Was the reign of Charles V the end of empire as people knew it? Robertson does not tell us. He adds to his

[22] D. Hume, *The History of England* (Charlottesville 2000:InteLex), *variorum edition*, F.L. van Holthoon ed., vol. 4, 355, record 9499.

[23] *William Robertson: View of the Progress in Europe*, F. Gilbert ed., (Chicago 1972: Chicago University Press).

[24] W. Robertson, *The History of the Reign of the Emperor Charles V* (London 1812: Cadell e.a.), x-xi.

discretion by ending his story more then a century before that system of balance came into being under William III, the stadholder-king.

d. *Gibbon*

Gibbon wrote a history of decline; so we cannot expect a theory of progress in his case. But a discussion of this work belongs in this essay for a reason he given himself:

> [A] philosopher may be permitted to enlarge his views, and to consider Europe as one great republic, whose various inhabitants have attained almost the same level of politeness and cultivation. The balance of power will continue to fluctuate, and the prosperity of our own, or the neighbouring kingdoms, may be alternately exalted or depressed; but these partial events cannot essentially injure our general state of happiness, the system of arts, and laws, and manners, which so advantageously distinguish, above the rest of mankind, the Europeans and their colonies.[25]

So Gibbon shares the view of his contemporaries that Europe as one republic, as a concert of nations, has become the pinnacle of civilization, and is there to stay. This was the favourite conclusion of the philosophers of the Enlightenment. Gibbon, like them, believed in the progress of civilization, but this also meant that the world after the Ancien Régime (here taken in the wider sense) would not substantially alter.

Now remarkably Gibbon does in no way refer to this European development. His *History* as a story of decline and fall is *the alternative* to that of modern Europe, and his leading thoughts are two:

1. His *History* closes the book of the Roman Empire as a viable regime.
2. No other people outside the Roman Empire were capable to rehabilitate the regime invented by the Roman citizens. Instead, under

[25] E. Gibbon, *The History of the Decline and Fall of the Roman Empire* (London 1995: Penguin, D.Womersley ed., II, 511; Gibbon uses <republic> for a regime that takes care of the welfare of its inhabitants and allow them a fair measure of freedom; not, in other words, as a regime without a king.

Edward Gibbon

Diocletianus, "Rome became", in the words of Patricia Craddock, "openly a monarchy in the Persian style."[26]

I shall elaborate on these conclusions in an Appendix attached to this essay, because my explanation will take up too much space here.

5. *Condorcet's Theory of Progress*

> Nos espérances sur l'état à venir de l'espèce humaine peuvent se réduire à ces trois points importants: la destruction de l'inégalité entre les nations; les progrès de l'égalité dans un même peuple; enfin le perfectionnement réel de l'homme.[27]

[26] P.B. Craddock, *Edward Gibbon, Luminous Historian, 1772-1794* (Baltimore 1989: John Hopkins University Press), 46-47.

[27] Condorcet, *Esquisse d'un Tableau Historique des Progrès de l'Esprit Humain* (Paris 1933: Boivin), 202.

This quotation is of interest for two reasons. First of all we have here a theory of progress which will lead mankind by necessity to a future with an open end; secondly it is typically a product of the revolutionary era. It emphasizes equality between men and nations. Equality was hardly discussed (except in the most abstract terms) during the Enlightenment.

Jean-Antoine Nicolas de Caritat, Marquis de Condorcet, wrote his *Esquisse* under threatening circumstances. He had to hide from the henchmen of Robespierre. He was betrayed and locked up, and the next morning he was found dead in his cell. Murder? Suicide? A heart attack? Nobody knows.

Condorcet's theory was that human inventions and discoveries will find their way to practical applications, and thus fuel progress. Invention and application are the two key elements of progress. Condorcet writes:

> … et, soit qu'on y rende compte d'une découverte, d'une théorie importante, d'un nouveau système de lois, d'une révolution politique, on s'occupera de déterminer quelles effets ont dû en résulter pour la portion la plus nombreuse de chaque société: car c'est là le véritable objet de la philosophie, puisque tous les effets intermediaires de ces même causes ne peuvent être regardés que comme des moyens d'agir enfin sur cette portion qui constitue vraiment la masse du genre humain.[28]

Condorcet believed in the revolution and it made him naïve. See the following quotation:

> Nous montrerons pourquoi les principes sur lesquels la constitution et les lois de la France ont été combinés, sont plus purs, plus précis, plus profonds, que ceux qui ont dirigé les Américains.[29]

After the brouhaha of many constitutions, the French Revolution temporarily settled down to a conservative regime, and it took as long

---

[28] Condorcet, *Esquisse,* 201-202.

[29] Condorcet, *Esquisse,* 172.

as the Third Republic (1875),[30] before the French accepted a regime they could live with. The American constitution gloriously withstood the test of time.

However, Condorcet was also a prophet. As David Williams remarks:

> The dynamics of progress that he elaborates in the *Esquisse* only really makes sense in the light of what he has to say about probability, actuarial science, rights, the civil order, justice, the constitutional process and human nature itself.[31]

Condorcet was one of the pioneers of the theory of probability. It made him aware of the possibility of predicting the unintended effects of inventions and, according to his theory of probability, these effects might become real. Hence he emphasized the necessary character of progress. He had the insight that, if you want progress, you must obey certain principles of justice, freedom and democracy. The first two were a legacy of the Enlightenment, the last mentioned was a product of the French Revolution. Condorcet looked to the individual, rather than to the collectivity, as the engine of progress.[32] So he was a liberal rather than a socialist. But both liberals and socialists were children of the French revolution. The ideological message of that revolution was that man could create his own world and Condorcet was it major messenger.

6. *The End of History*

The end of history is a concept, which Fukuyama borrowed from Hegel and, since then, has been sensible enough to retract. It means that the future will hold no more surprises, if nations stick to principles of free trade and peaceful negotiation. When applied to Hume, the idea is that you will have political stability if the partners in a

[30] In 1875 the national assembly voted against re-installing the monarchy with a majority of one vote and opted for the republic which was there to stay.

[31] D. Williams, *Condorcet and Modernity* (Cambridge 2004: Cambridge University Press), 9.

[32] K.M. Baker, *Condorcet. From Natural Philosophy to Social Mathematics* (Chicago 1975: Chicago University Press), 120.

mixed government conclude a pact of mutual non-interference. The end of history in Hume's case has the implication that there is no room for a parliamentary democracy, which depends on osmosis of the executive and legislative branch of government. The concept is not applicable to a *philosophe* like Voltaire. The most remarkable thing about philosophy as political science in the French Enlightenment is that it is not there. It is amazing how ill prepared Frenchmen were at the eve of the Revolution. Even when the decision was taken to convene the *États Généraux* after more than 150 years, no one had a firm idea of how to reform this rickety institution. The end of history in the French case must indicate that, for the *philosophes*, it was inconceivable that the Ancien Régime could disappear and the *société des ordres* with it. So there was no fertile ground for a theory of progress.

In the nineteenth century two dynamic forces fuelled the theory of progress. One was the ideology that we can create a just and free society. The other force is the Industrial Revolution, that started to change society and political relations in an unprecedented way. Comte, Marx, Spencer: we witness a great number of theories of progress in this century. All the reformers shared the illusion that mankind would be able to use economic developments for the benefit of their theories. Moral progress would control technical progress. John Stuart Mill, a strong believer in moral progress, warned in 1848 that, if Englishmen were not able to regulate their number of children, economic competition would remain a rat race without purpose. He was the first to face the prospect of a stationary state with equanimity.[33] Some forty years later the Industrial Revolution started to effect nations and peoples on a global scale, and then it became evident that population growth could not only be a brake on growth, but one of its causes. Now, 160 years later again, few observers still have the illusion that economic growth will *automatically* lead to moral progress. The problem has become how we can stop economic growth in its present form. Perhaps our present predicament makes it of some interest to

[33] F.L. van Holthoon, *The Road to Utopia. A Study of John Stuart Mill's Social Thought* (Assen 1971: van Gorcum), ch. 6, "Improvement and Wealth. A Case for the Stationary State".

study the philosophers of the Enlightenment who believed in moral improvement while things remain as they are.

Gibbon's *History of the Decline and Fall*. An appendix

Let me repeat the quotation which I gave in the preceding essay to indicate that Gibbon firmly believed in the central tenets of the Enlightenment:

> [A] philosopher may be permitted to enlarge his views, and to consider Europe as one great republic, whose various inhabitants have attained almost the same level of politeness and cultivation. The balance of power will continue to fluctuate, and the prosperity of our own, or the neighbouring kingdoms, may be alternately exalted or depressed; but these partial events cannot essentially injure our general state of happiness, the system of arts, and laws, and manners, which so advantageously distinguish, above the rest of mankind, the Europeans and their colonies.[34]

And the last sentence of his *General Observations on the Fall of the Roman Empire in the West*, which ends book three reads:

> We may therefore[35] acquiesce in the pleasing conclusion, that every age of the world has increased, and still increases, the real wealth, the happiness, the knowledge, and perhaps the virtue, of the human race.[36]

Gibbon shared the idea of Enlightened progress and, like his fellow writers, he held the complacent view that, since Europe had come this far, things would stay as they are. Like Voltaire, Goguet, de Guignes and other writers, other civilizations had added to the progress of arts and sciences but, at present, there was no viable seat of civiliza-

---

[34] E. Gibbon, *The History of the Decline and Fall of the Roman Empire* (London 1995: Penguin, D.Womersley ed., II, 511. Gibbon uses <republic> for a regime that takes care of the welfare of its inhabitants and allows them a fair measure of freedom; not, in other words, as a regime without a king.

[35] <Therefore> refers to Gibbon's observation that the inventions and achievements never get lost.

[36] E. Gibbon, *The History of the Decline and Fall*, II, p. 516.

tion, alternate to that of eighteenth-century Europe. And, as to the Roman Empire, they could destroy it, but could not replace its civilizational order. The days of the Roman republican freedom are over. In a heated conversation with the Abbé de Mably, who extolled the idea of virtue as portrayed by Livius, Gibbon "defended generally the monarchical government."[37] Like Voltaire, Hume and many others he saw monarchy as the regime most convenient to eighteenth-century civil society.

Why then did Gibbon write a history of decline and avoided to discuss any signs of progress in European history? As I pointed out in my preceding essay, his history of decline is an alternative to how we usually write European history since the fall of the Roman empire in the West. And why did he not end his story in 476? The more so as Gibbon writes that the "story of its ruin is simple and obvious".[38] Why pursue the story of the Byzantine empire for another thousand years, "a story which is a "tedious and uniform tale of weakness and misery"?[39] The answer to these questions is that, how Gibbon wrote his history of decline, tells why he did write it. The general caption of John Pocock's five volumes dealing with Gibbon's works – *Barbarism and Religion* - is useful in dealing with this answer.

What about religion? The ending chapters (15 and 16) in the first volume were published in 1776. In them Gibbon discussed the rise of early Christianity, and so created a bitter controversy with the British clergy. Gibbon's main point (mentioned earlier) was that he wanted to give a wholly secular description of that history and, even if he had tried (which he did not), he could not avoid the conclusion to be

[37] P. Craddock, *Edward Gibbon*, p. 96. She quotes the report by Godin de la Brenellerie.

[38] E. Gibbon, *The History of the Decline and Fall*, vol. 2 "General Observations", 509. Steve Runciman remarks, about Gibbon's gloomy picture of the Byzantine Empire: "The arrogant autocracy with its servile subjects which Gibbon attributed to Byzantium never in fact existed", S. Runciman, "Gibbon and Byzantium", *Edward Gibbon and the Decline and Fall of the Roman Empire* (Cambridge Mass. 1977: Harvard University Press), G.W. Bowersock e.o. eds, 59.

[39] E. Gibbon, *The History of Decline and Fall*, vol. 3, ch. 48, p. 23.

drawn by his readers, that Christian history as the story of God's providence, *l'histoire sacrée*, was no longer valid. That was one of the main messages of the Enlightenment and had been -as we have seen– the guiding perspective of Voltaire's *Essay sur les Moeurs*. Hume's *Natural History of Religion*, which Gibbon knew very well, did not even deign to make the point that there could be a sacred history.[40]

Now Hume was the great infidel, according to the Christian ministers who attacked Gibbon's history of early Christianity, and they thought that Hume's theory, that the source of religion was fear for the unknown, was absurd anyway. However, Gibbon's analysis came too close to their own doubts to the story of the *histoire sacrée*. And hence some of them reacted so violently, particularly because Gibbon added irony as an insult to the injury of his masterly secular version.[41]

Pocock has pointed out that chapters 15 and 16 are "departures" from his main concern about the influence of Christianity on the decline of the Roman Empire.[42] More important in this respect is chapter 28 in which Gibbon related the ruin of paganism under Theodosius. Senator Symmachus made an impassioned appeal for the maintenance of the pagan rites. He argued "that the Roman sacrifices would be deprived of their force and energy, if they were no longer celebrated at the expence, as well as in the name, of the republic."[43] Yet paganism with its statues and temples was eradicated from public life, and with it went the Roman conception of patriotism. Instead, the official church went on to incorporate pagan superstition with its veneration of saints.

[40] Hume's *Dialogues Concerning Natural Religion* was only published three years after the publication of Gibbon's first volume, in 1779. See for the reactions to Hume's NHR T.L. Beauchamp, "The Reception of the Natural History of Religion", in his edition of *The Natural History of Religion* (Oxford 2007: Clarendon Press), cxxi ff.

[41] I mentioned dr Watson's reaction in my essay on Deism. His reaction was courteous, but to the point. If Gibbon did not want to discuss God as the primary cause of the rise of Christianity, there was no possibility that he and Hume could reach an agreement on the proper story of early Christianity.

[42] J.G.A. Pocock, *Barbarism and Religion*, vol. 5, *Religion: The First Triumph* (Cambridge 2010: Cambridge University Press), p. 306.

[43] E. Gibbon, *History of the Decline and Fall*, vol. II, ch. 28, p. 75.

> The religion of Constantine achieved, in less than a century, the final conquest of the Roman empire, but the victors themselves were insensibly subdued by the arts of their vanquished rivals.[44]

As a consequence, the Roman Empire turned into an oriental despotism by its fusion of polity and church. The Roman citizens of the republic had interpreted freedom as the patriotic duty to defend their city. In the reign of Theodosius that kind of republican freedom only existed in name, but now they also lost the other freedom: the freedom of thought. The Roman form of oriental despotism lived on in the Byzantine Empire till the fall of Constantinople. "Rome became openly a monarchy in the Persian Style", as Craddock observes in relation to the reign of Diocletianus.[45] The Roman Empire joined the eastern empires, but lacked the military strength of these empires.

And the Pocock's caption of barbarism? In chapter 2 Gibbon described the "Union and internal Prosperity of the Roman Empire in the Age of the Antonines". It was what Pocock calls the "Antonine Moment" in Roman history. The Empire had secure borders, an efficient government and strong armies at the borders. Communications were excellent and trade and agriculture prospered. And then with Commodus the rot set in and in the end:

> The army was licentious without spirit, the nation turbulent without freedom: the Barbarians of the East and West pressed on the monarchy, and the loss of the provinces was terminated by the final servitude of the capital.[46]

Gibbon used the term barbarism as a generic notion for those who attacked and tried to destroy the civilized life of the Roman Empire.[47] So the barbarians included the Germanic tribes, the Huns, the Persians, and later on the Tartars and the Arabs. In fact Gibbon's relation of Byzantine history tends to be short and even perfunctory. Instead,

---

[44] E. Gibbon, *The History of the Decline and Fall*, vol. II, ch. 28, p. 97.

[45] P. Craddock, *Edward Gibbon,* 46-47.

[46] E. Gibbon, *The History of the Decline and Fall*, vol. 3, ch. 48, p. 85.

[47] Consequently he also regarded the crusaders as barbarians. *The Decline anf Fall of the Roman Empire*, vol. 3, ch. 58.

he has long chapters on the Arabs and their conquests, the Bulgarians, Zingis Khan and Tamerlane (or Timour), and of course Mahomed II, who eventually conquered Constantinople. Gibbon was impressed by the achievements of these princes, but his verdict of Tamerlane stands for them all: "If some partial disorders, some local oppressions, were healed by the sword of Timour, the remedy was far more pernicious than the disease".[48] His conquests destroyed old states without replacing them with a new order and, if his reign had any benefits, these evaporated at his death. The object lesson of his story is that *Tamerlane's regime was inherently unstable and could never create a new Antonine Moment within the Roman Empire.* And what applies to the Tartars applies to the Turks. The Ottoman Empire was much more stable, but Gibbon's portrait of Mahomed II is as unflattering as that of Tamerlane.[49] He was a military despot and everything remained the property of Mahomed II and his successors. *They could replace the military strength of the Roman Empire, but not its civilization.* So here we have the reason why Gibbon wrote his story at great length and focussed exclusively on the decline of the Empire. He wanted to make it absolutely clear that the Roman Empire could not be resurrected. That was his message to his contemporaries.The alternative for Europe had to come from the balance of power between nations.

So the Christian religion, particularly as state religion, was a cause of weakness, and the barbarian attacks made it impossible to maintain order and civilization within in the Empire. Perhaps the fundamental cause of the decline came from Rome's expansion from a city-state into an empire. In his *Discorsi* Machiavelli had suggested that the constitution of the city state was not suitable for an expansion by conquest and Montesquieu added to this the notion that the internal dissension between the tribunes and the senate caused disorder in the late republic. Gibbon included all these explanations in his story. It could be that one of the reasons why he added another thousand years after the fall of Rome in 476 is that he wanted to show that a military regime such as the Roman Republic, afterwards Empire, is an inher-

48 E. Gibbon, *The History of the Decline and Fall*, vol. 3, ch. 65, p. 851.

49 E. Gibbon, *The Decline and Fall*, vol. 3, ch. 68, p. 935.

ently unstable regime. If this was his intention, he did not theorize about it, but told its story.

In his chapter "Autobiography in Time of Revolution"[50] David Womerley analysed six drafts of Gibbon's *Autobiography*, which his friend Lord Sheffield used to assemble a memoir after Gibbon's death. Womersley gives the reason why Gibbon hesitated to publish his autobiography in his lifetime. He had read Burke's *Reflections on the Revolution in France* (1790). He was deeply impressed by Burke's argument that a just regard for the established religion is essential for the well-being of society. In draft E - which he intended to publish himself but could not because he died in the meantime – Gibbon toned down his involvement with the French *philosophes* and retouched his motives for writing the chapters on early Christianity. As I read Womersley's analysis it is the story of a stalemate. Gibbon could not really undo his reputation as a critic of Christianity, but in vain he tried to make room for a Burkean analysis of organic change.

To me the interest about Gibbon's memoirs is that he must have realized that the French Revolution had shattered his confident idea of a concert of European nations, which – see the peace plan of the Abbé de St. Pierre – depended on the Ancien Régimes of pre-revolutionary Europe. Gibbon had written the story of the end of classical Empire realizing, after he had finished it, that, given the events of the French Revolution, he no longer knew what would replace it. Gibbon is often regarded as the first historist historian, and he earned this qualification because of his brilliant gift of collating disparate facts into a convincing story. In this respect he was only rivalled by Leopold von Ranke among the nineteenth-century historians. Gibbon obeyed Ranke's dictum that "Jede Epoch ist unmittelbar zu Gott" before it was even written down. He ended his *Epoch* in convincing style.

---

[50] D. Womerley, *Gibbon and the 'Watchmen of the Holy City, the Historian and his Reputation, 1776-1815*, (Oxford 2002: Clarendon Press), 207 ff.

X. Back to the Enlightenment?

The Enlightenment became a label in the nineteenth century because of its association with technical progress. The Enlightenment became an agenda for the demands of man in the modern world. The ideas of the eighteenth-century Enlightenment in their new setting lost the charm of their original formulation and gave a false idea of what the philosophers of the Enlightenment were after. We cannot pretend to become eighteenth-century philosophers again, but a reflection on their ideas in their original setting may help us to cope with our own problems.

1. *Introduction*

The historian must try to present as authentic a picture of the past he is studying as he can. In the history of ideas that is a particularly difficult task. We use more or less the same words as our eighteenth-century ancestors, but they often don't mean the same thing, not quite. This is because these words refer to a social context, which is not ours anymore. What the historian must do is to turn the familiar into the unfamiliar. This is the case with the ideas of the Enlightenment.

The Enlightenment was not the age of reason, if we mean by it that science tells us how to conduct our lives. It should rather be considered the age of reasonableness and as reasonableness is a passion – at least if Hume is right - that explains why the philosophers of the Enlightenment paid so much attention to sentiment. The study of sentiment was part of their scientific outlook. Those who ignore the fact that the Enlightenment is also the age of sentiment will not be able to understand it.

The philosophers of the Enlightenment have the reputation of being anti-religious and anti-church. However, I hope to have made it clear that, though in Catholic countries they usually were anti-church, nowhere were they anti-religious. The conflict between philosophers and the clergy was rather that the former advocated a purely secular morality that did not depend on the prescription of the churches. That conflict was about power and it made the philosophers circumspect in bringing their message, because they knew that the clergy had control over the common people and they had not. Though they did not believe in the miracles, the churches taught they respected the authority of these institutions, even if not for their own persons. It was given to nineteenth-century rationalists, such as Auguste Comte, to insist on the unconditional authority of reason, even to the extent that he erected a new religion on the basis of it.

The philosophers of the Enlightenment believed in freedom of thought and expression, though they accepted certain, conventional, conditions of restraint. Political freedom was another matter. Liberty of the press? Certainly, but even in Britain those in favour of this freedom accepted certain limitations to what the press could publish. Voting rights? Universal suffrage for men, let alone for women, was beyond the mental horizon of any eighteenth-century literate person. The heart of the matter is that these philosophers accepted the society of orders as their point of departure for any of the reforms they had in mind. And that fact alone explains the watershed that exists between the Enlightenment and the century that followed.

Can we turn back to the Enlightenment? Of course we cannot. To mention only one thing: the common people, marginalized in the Ancien Regime, have become part of civil society and want to be heard. Their incorporation within society is no mean achievement and it precludes any reference to the society of orders, that the philosophers of the Enlightenment took for granted. So we could not get back to the eighteenth-century, even if we wished and of course we don't want to. It was in many ways a cruel century. It stank, literally. For emotional and material reasons we would not feel comfortable in that century.

The nineteenth century is the era of great change and that change has effected the reception of the Enlightenment in that century. The Enlightenment became a label for advocates and critics. Those who

Leopold von Ranke

argued for it saw enlightenment values as the only way to cope with the great change. Those who were against that change rejected these values as a matter of course. An early enemy of the Enlightenment was Isaac da Costa, in his *Bezwaren tegen de Geest der Eeuw* ["Objections against the Spirit of the Century"]. Interestingly da Costa called his age (the early nineteenth-century) 'the age of enlightenment', and so it was equivalent to the age of slavery and superstition, in which "every raw and uncooked plan for improvement" is launched.[1] Da Costa defended the traditional Christian faith. So he was a man from the right. However, there have also been critics of the Enlightenment on the left. The most peculiar example of this criticism is Max Horkheimer and Theodor Adorno's *Dialektik der Aufklärung.* In this joint publication, published in Amsterdam in 1947, they regard fas-

[1] "Ieder raauw en ongekookt ontwerp van verbetering", I. da Costa, *Bezwaren tegen den Geest der Eeuw,* (1823) (Leiden 1923: Sijthoff), 37.

cism as the corrupted product of the Enlightenment, but the corruption does not stop with the defeat of fascism, as becomes clear from the first sentence of their book:

> Seit je hat Aufklärung im umfassendsten Sinn fortschreitenden Denkens das Ziel verfolgt, von den Menschen die Furcht zu nehmen und sie als Herren einzusetzen. Aber die vollends aufgeklärte Erde strahlt im Zeichen triumphalen Unheils. Das Programm der Aufklärung war die Entzauberung der Welt.[2]

This quotation refers to the future. Evidently fascism was only one step on the road to ruin.

What was their objection to the Enlightenment? According to them the slogan of the Enlightenment for knowledge insists on applied, instrumental knowledge, and that creates a one-dimensional reality of business and cheap recreation.[3] Applied science, furthermore, creates endless possibilities for manipulation, which the fascists were great in exploiting. Horkheimer and Adorno's complaint is that the Enlightenment has created a flattened reality in which means and not purpose prevails. So in their view the Enlightenment has become the ally of the Industrial Revolution and of the world it has created. So for critics from the right and the left as well as for advocates of the Enlightenment in the nineteenth century (and after) the concept got a dynamic character and so could create the suggestion that the eighteenth-century philosophers of the Enlightenment were the pathfinders of the social, economic and political changes in the centuries to come.

Discussing Gibbon's *History* I quoted Ranke's dictum "Jede Epoche is unmittelbar zu Gott". The French Revolution closed the period of the Enlightenment in a Rankian sense, and the fascinating and

---

[2] M. Horkheimer & Th.W. Adorno, *Dialektik der Aufklärung, Philosophische Fragmente* (Frankfurt a. M. 1984: Fischer), p. 7.

[3] It was Herbert Marcuse, as them a member of the Frankfurter School, who invented the term one-dimensional man. See H. Marcuse, *One Dimensional Man* (London 1968: Sphere books).

peculiar fact is that we have not reached a new period, because the Industrial Revolution is still a story without ending.

2. *The Ideology of Planning Society*

The ideas of the French Revolution had a great influence on the nineteenth-century debate, and that was remarkable because the quality of these ideas was poor. There was no match between constitutional proposals and political reality. William Sewell writes about Siéyès:

> However desirable the wholesale abolition of privilege [on 4 August 1789] may have seemed to him in retrospect, it was an unanticipated consequence of *What is the Third Estate?* and not the fulfilment of a conscious plan.[4]

Indeed, Siéyès wrote constitutions without having an idea of how they could fit the present political situation. When asked what he had done during the period of the Terror, he replied: I survived. That was his most sensible remark. Robespierre joined the Revolution coming from Arras as a supporter of the monarchy, and he was against the death penalty. He became the architect of the Terror and the hangman (or rather the headman) during that period. He evidently was a prisoner of events, and his growing paranoia motivated him to instigate the great cleanup of all the persons and factions who were against the Revolution. Revolution to the revolutionaries meant spring cleaning starting with abolishing history, and that attempt was enough to alarm Edmund Burke and justly so. For, abolishing history also means eliminating the rule of law by way of improvisation.

Many plans for the reconstruction of society were produced in the nineteenth-century. Comte, Marx and Spencer made them, and their plans had a willful disregard in common for the political measures and the political philosophy that were needed to put them into practice. Reading Lenin's *State and Revolution* I was bothered by his

[4] W.H. Sewell Jr., *A Rhetoric of Bourgeois Revolution, the Abbé Sieyes and What is the Third Estate?* (Durham 1994: Duke University Press), 144.

solution to the problem the revolution would create.[5] How is it that an intelligent man like Lenin could maintain that you could run Russia as a post office? This must have been propaganda, you are inclined to think, but there may have been a worse explanation and this is that Lenin believed what he wrote. In that case the Russians paid a heavy price for Lenin's naivety.

Revolutionary thinking is the ideology of planning a frictionless society, so that the state is not needed anymore, except for locking up criminals. The sad thing, of course, is that planning can never be frictionless and that you need democracy to repair the mistakes. The political reality of Soviet Russia was that Stalin and a small elite of communist officials forced through 'solutions' with a total disregard for human lives.

However, not only the communists were the victim of the ideology of planning society. Liberals (including reformist socialists for the sake of the argument) trusted that the equilibrium of supply and demand would solve most of their economic problems, and that the margin which economic growth created could be used for social reforms. Liberals and, certainly, socialists, believed in the role of the state, but in a curious way they relied on economic forces to make their policies possible. However, in this way they underestimated the unpredictable outcome of these economic forces, which in fact reduced their planning to damage control.

In the fifties of the twentieth century, policy makers thought they had discovered the magic formula: economic growth. With Keynes they said that it does not matter whether we divide the cake in equal parts as long as the growing size of the cake allows us to give everyone a larger share than he had before. Economic growth will undoubtedly create inflation, but as long as that inflation is moderate and wages will exceed prices, everyone can be happy, including officials and politicians, because the real value of the debt of the state will diminish.

---

[5] W.J. Lenin, "The State and Revolution, The Marxist Theory of the State and the Task of the Proletariate in the Revolution", *Coll. Works* (Moskou 1974: Progress).

Robespierre

This magic formula worked more or less until the credit crisis of 2008. That crisis shattered the belief that in principle the economies of the world would grow by a gradual process, and commentators were shocked to learn that economic growth since the very beginning of economic expansion had created a highly unstable global economy. Since the fall of the Berlin wall in 1989, the liberal and socialist pragmatists had the final say, and they scorned the Russians who had made a mess of things. But are the pragmatists doing so much better? If we look back to the crisis of 2008 the most disconcerting fact of that crisis is that none of the experts saw it coming. And the second disconcerting fact is that they still talk about economic growth as a remedy for the aftermath of the 2008 crisis. And yet they should know that economic growth, whatever its short term merits, is not the solution for creating a more stable global economy.

In the meantime we have got another problem. We almost literally are consuming mother earth. The depletion of our resources together with the global warming created by the exhaust of CO_2 may threaten humankind in the foreseeable future. The unintended effects of the sum total of our activities are so dangerous, because they are not captured within our schemes of control. We need long term strategies to deal with these externalities. In the meantime we are well advised to follow Stuart Mill's advice and concentrate on the division of the cake we have and not on the one we plan to create.

3. *The Great Change: Modernization*

Who would draw the conclusion that modern humans are a collection of bunglers is wrong, of course. Human achievements in building the world we know have been colossal in technical, social and economic terms. Not so much in political terms, I am afraid. One might think that war as a solution to conflict would become an obsolete measure since the beginning of the Industrial Revolution, because that Revolution thrives by cooperation not conflict. Enlightenment, we might say, means closing the gap between political decision making and the reality of human cooperation. But how? In fact we are incapable of doing so, and perhaps it is not so strange that we don't know how to deal with the world we ourselves are creating. The great change unleashed by the Industrial Revolution has created what Jan Romein has called 'the deviation from the universal human pattern' ["de afwijking van het Algemeen Menselijk Patroon"].[6] Whether such a universal parttern ever existed is a matter for debate, but that everyone everwhere has been and is being confronted by an emerging world which in no way matches their life, experiences and customs, is a fact. Furthermore the great change prevents us, citizens of the world, from getting accustomed to our present situation, because the future is always full of surprises.

[6] J. Romein, *Aera van Europa. De Eropese Geschiedenis en de Afwijking van het Algemeen Menselijk atroon* (Leiden 1954: Brill).

J. M. Keynes

The world is in a state of constant flux, because of what we might call the process of modernization. To be modern means that we keep up to date and view everything, even from our immediate past, with suspicion. New car models and articles of fashion are modern, but the term also applies to bureaucratic instructions and new policies. Being modern means that we have to adapt to these new instructions and policies, which tomorrow may again be out of date and the day after tomorrow have been forgotten. The Now is modern and the process, which gets us there constantly, puts at risk what we have acquired and achieved.

What we have achieved is impressive, but in what we have achieved the commands of economic necessity at least are as important as our plans and intentions. Friedrich Engels wrote to a friend:

> Es ist nicht, dass die oekonomische Lage *Ursache, allein aktiv* ist und alle andere nur passive Wirkung. Sondern es ist die Wech-

> selwirkung auf Grundlage der in *letzter Instanz* stets sich durchsetzenden oekonomischen Notwendigkeit.[7]

Feminists have fought a heroic battle for equal rights at the ballot and on the shopfloor. Because they had to work as Rosie the riveter during World War One, they got the voting rights and the labour market has decided that the talents of women are needed in the production of services and goods. And so couples raising a family have had to adapt their respective roles. That often has not been easy, but the point is that they must.

We can describe the characteristics of the process of modernization in six points.

a. *Technical Inventions*

In the beginning technical change became visible in canals, paved roads, textile machines, Watt's steam engine, and factories. Now it manifests itself in new means of communication and the electronic innovation which backs it up. The classical economists explained the growth of the economy by the interplay of soil, labour and capital, the classical factors of production. Now they are no longer the main causes of economic growth, as Schumpeter has argued with forceful arguments.[8] Innovations push the economy forward. The economy constantly has the tendency to reach equilibrium and, as a consequence, profits tend to diminish to the rate of interest. That tendency is interrupted by innovations which, during a certain period, tend to raise profits to a spectacular height for those who control these inventions. For those who view uncontrollable modernization with some concern inventions may be regarded as a mixed blessing.

---

[7] *Marx-Engels Werke* (Berlin 1956: Dietz), 39, 206; cited in F.L. van Holthoon, *Het Gebruik van het Woord Ideologie bij Engels en Marx* (Groningen 1973: Tjeenk Willink) [Inaugural].

[8] Schumpeter wrote a lot on this subject; the essential text is *Business Cycles* (1939) (Philadelphia 1982: Porcupine Press).

b. *Economic Growth*

In the sixties of the last century Walt Rostow published his *Stages of Economic Growth.*[9] He took the Industrial Revolution in England as his model to explain how the economy took off at a certain moment, broke through the ceiling of the traditional economy, to reach eventually a stage of maturity, in which economic growth became a self-propelling force, and in which growth would generate new growth. Rostow maintained that the British example was repeated on the continent. After the publication of the book, there occurred a lively debate on patterns of growth and about the question whether all regions outside Europe and America could participate in the process. No one questioned the fact of what Rostow called sustained growth: at least until the Club of Rome published its *Limits of Growth*, a report in which they predicted that the scarcity of fossil fuel would bring the economy to a standstill.[10] They were wrong. In the past two hundred and fifty years the economies of the Western world have grown at an exponential rate and more recently countries in Asia, South America and Africa have joined the club. And notwithstanding the present crisis there are no reasons to expect the ending of economic growth on a global scale. The question rather is at what cost we are creating this economic growth. Economic growth is measured by comparing gross national products of this year to those of a former year. The problem with this measurement is that it includes polluting activities as earnings adding to the national income, and that it disregards externalities. To name but one: all the peoples of the world have become richer than they were (statistically not necessarily as individuals), but the number of human beings is still increasing at a rate which makes us ask how long mother earth can sustain this growing population.

9 W. Rostow, *The Stages of Economic Growth* (Cambridge 1960:Cambridge University Press).

10 D. Meadows et al., *The Limits of Growth* (London 1972: Earth Island) and D. Meadows, *Limits to the Growth, the 30 Year Update* (London 2005: Earthscan).

c. *The Rationalization of Norms*

A modern organization needs formal rules to be able to function. Human transactions have become more frequent and complicated, and with them the role of government has grown. Bureacratization is, as Max Weber has explained, the other face of rationalization. Rules should be predictable and acceptable to human groups with different beliefs and lifestyles.

So, we have to introduce rules which can mediate between these different beliefs and lifestyles, and rationalization tries to introduce a neutral element in the way we judge actions. In doing so it has transformed our public morality. We tend to judge actions by their consequences rather than by the intentions of the actors. If consequences add to the sum of happiness we approve them, if they diminish the sum we condemn them.

However, as individuals our personal happiness also relies on our motives for undertaking a certain action, and so there may occur a conflict between our intentions and the way the consequences of our actions are judged in society (and particularly by policy makers). Now, one may argue that the conflict between intentions and consequences is always present, but the conflict becomes serious when only consequences are acceptable as the norm of judging actions. That will mean the frustration of personal happiness. Adam Smith and David Hume did not know this conflict, because they argued that only the quality of intentions can decide whether an action is moral or not.[11]

d. *From an Ascribed to an Achieved Status*

On this subject I can be brief. Modern society has a demand for well-educated persons, who manage to perform complicated tasks. So family origin and ascribed status no longer are the deciding factors in making careers, but merit is. And so status is largely based on merit in modern society, or at least on perceived merit.

[11] See F.L. van Holthoon, "Sympathy and Utility, a Comparison of the Moral Philosophy of Hume and Smith", *2000. The European Journal*, X(1), 2009.

e. *The Widening Scale of Human Relations*

It is an expression I used in a book on social history to describe the modern situation of mankind.[12] It means that no one is locked up anymore in his local situation, and can now communicate and do business with the world, and today even from his home. This is undoubtedly a positive thing. Yet we are also part of what David Riesman called the lonely crowd.[13] As individuals, we are alone in a mass of people which we do not know on a face to face relationship. More than a century before Riesman, Tocqueville used the fact that we are losing out on the intermediate relations between the state and the individual, to describe the state as an all-powerful and tutelary institution. Since his death in 1859, trade unions and political parties have fulfilled this intermediate role with great effect though, more recently, they have lost most of their lustre. Whether these organisations will be able to reinvent their roles, remains to be seen. In the meantime the mobile phone and the internet has become a powerful tool in the hands of the home sitter. At home he can urge his fellows to man the squares venting their frustrations with the existing government. How we will be able to square this new political phenomenon with our existing constitutional practices remains for the present an open question.

f. *The Evaporation of Tradition*

Until recently the Christian churches in the West had a tremendous hold on individuals and regulated their behaviour. The most sensational outcome of modernization is that people, at least in the West, do not listen to the churches anymore. The emptying of the Christian churches is part of the encompassing process of the loss or, as I called it, the evaporation of tradition. Take this example: historically Western society had a patriarchical character. Gradually paternal authority

---

[12] F.L. van Holthoon, *Mensen in Europa* (Alphen a.d., Rijn 1977: Samsom), 101.

[13] D. Riesman, *The Lonely Crowd. A Study of the Changing American Character* (New Haven 1950: Yale University Press).

has been whittled down by the ideological and economic forces associated with modernization. Public morality in the Western world is being under the sway of utilitarian considerations. Some practices, strongly condemned by the churches, such as those attached to sexuality, are left to the discretion of individuals, because they are not relevant for the functioning of society. Others are insisted on as dysfunctional or worse, such as smoking, which is considered detrimental to the non-smoker. Or take racism or any other form of discrimination, which is condemned because it spoils social relations. Many will think that these habits or practices are simply deplorable, but the arguments to act against them are always utlitarian.

If we look at the world of Islam, we can notice how invasive and aggressive this consequential utilitarianism can become. It will be of interest to see how the world of Islam will cope with this aspect of modernization which insists that their women should be free to pursue their lives in the way they want (or rather in the way we in the West think they want) and which forces moslims to be tolerant to non- believers. And how sincere are those in the West who accept that homosexuals should be able to lead normal lives? Do they really believe that homosexual behaviour is none of their business or are they being politically correct, secretly thinking that homosexuality is abhorrent? The point is that public morality in its utilitarian version forces them to be tolerant even if they are not.

These five points describe modernization in its tendencies and outcomes and the overall point of modernization is that it forces us to do things and to accept things whether we like them or not.

4. *Eros and Thanatos*

A few years ago I wrote a survey of political theories in the nineteenth-century Western world. Its subtitle was *Theories, Illusions, Realities.* My conclusions were that there are no political theories anymore, but that political science dealt with the nuts and bolts of politics. A common illusion was that we can do without the state or at most the state will only need to function as Carlyle's famous night-watch. And the reality has been that the state as an institution became more powerful than ever before. An interesting aspect of this survey was that the most original theories did not deal with politics proper, but with human fate in a situation of change. The names of Marx, Durkheim, Max Weber and Freud were associated with these theories. Their perspective on the fate of modern man was gloomy. H. Stuart Hughes wrote a magnificent book on their ideas, *Consciousness and Society*, and its subtitle *The Reorientation of European Thought* is revealing.[14] These four thinkers became the founders of the new discipline of sociology, and the new discipline was meant to teach individuals how to survive under the conditions of modernity.

According to the young Marx, individuals have become alienated in the course of economic development. In an argument which echoes Rousseau's notion that civilization corrupts man, human beings are the victims of the division of labour. In the course of that process individuals lose their identity and become subjected to the economic machinery. The mature Marx introduces the notion that bourgeois capitalism is creating an unstable economic structure. Adam Smith is wrong. Instead of equilibrium economic development leads us up a spiral staircase which has an explosion at an end, the big *Kladderadatsch*, as Marx called it. In the long run the communist utopia will present permanent bliss, but in the meantime human beings in capitalist society are the prisoners of their drive for change.[15]

The Calvinist who, according to Max Weber, is the prototype of modern man, builds an iron cage for himself. He wants to serve God by his work and creates a Godless world. That is a world of bureaucratic rules in which rationalization reigns supreme and the world as it was known has lost its magic charm. Weber's way out of boredom was dedication to the German nation. During world war one, when he noticed the pipe-dreams of German hegemony, he became disabused.

[14] (New York 1958: Vintage).

[15] Talcott Parsons distilled from these gloomy analyses a much more optimistic view of modern society. His voluntaristic theory sketches a structure based on functional relations, which need little intervention by the state. See Talcott Parsons, *The Structure of Social Action* (Glencoe 1949: Free Press); also F.L. van Holthoon, *State and Civil Society*, 334 ff.

Sigmund Freud

In the lecture *Politik als Beruf* delivered in München in 1919 for a student audience he held a funeral oration on German nationalism. It was a grim message. Politics could only mean a responsible way on how to deal with evil.

Durkheim's idea of *anomie* is not so easy to understand. It means that a curious lawless state of mind occurs because people have too many options. They do no longer know what to choose and so lose their sense for the limits of things, because they think they can have everything they want. This *embarrass du choix* does not turn individuals into criminals, but they lose their moral sense, and utility becomes a matter of policy rather than of motives. The equation is that more wealth means that it becomes more difficult for the individual to make responsible choices.

This paragraph carries the title of two concepts, which Freud developed in his essay *Das Unbehagen in der Kultur*, better known in its English translation *Civilisation and it Discontents.* Modern development creates a state of permanent discontent in individuals. Freud writes:

> How has it happened that so many people have come to take up this strange attitude of hostility to civilization? I believe that the basis of it was a deep and long-standing dissatisfaction with the then existing state of civilization, and that on that basis a condemnation of it was built up, occasioned by certain specific events.

Modern science presents us with luxury and comfort, bu otherwise is not helpful:

> The fulfilment of a longing that goes back thousands of years, has not increased the amount of pleasurable satisfaction which they may expect from life, and has not made them feel happier.[16]

Freud spent his last years as a refugee in London and had time to reflect on the horrors of World War One and the new horrors Nazism was creating. Why it is that man has this senseless urge to annihilate his fellow human beings? Freud answered that man is discontented and bored under the conditions of the modern world. He has two basic drives. *Eros* does make him seek friendship and love, but when he is deeply frustrated he switches to *thanatos*, his second drive. *Thanatos* is the drive to annihilate others, particularly those over whom he has absolute power. It seems to me that the terrorist who blows himself up is the ultimate example of someone motivated by *thanatos*. He not only wants to destroy others, but demonstrates that he does not want to be on this earth any more.

Perhaps the most disturbing thought we can associate with Freud's analysis is that the terrorist is lurking in all of us. In this sense the German title is better than the English one. Modernization causes a faint sense of discomfort in our souls. Few of us will be willing to adopt extreme measures on the basis of this *Unbehagen*; some may be willing to act as the shield without which terrorists cannot act.

[16] S. Freud, "Civilization and its Discontents", *The Freud Reader* (London 1995: Vintage), P.Gay ed., 735-736.

5. *The Privileged Moment*

Marvin Becker used the term 'a privileged moment' to indicate the emergence of civil society in Scotland, England and France.[17] That is a well-chosen term, which could be applied to the Enlightenment as a whole. The philosophers of the Enlightenment were expecting a world of peaceful cooperation in which enlightenment would induce the civilized behaviour necessary for the purpose. Their privilege was that they could think about civilized behaviour without taking into account the common people and the industrial change which would promote their cause.

Their common purpose was what Siep Stuurman has called the meta-concept of common humanity, and they were the first to claim that they could adapt the social order to the reforms they had in mind.[18] We cannot have their privilege of composure, because our social order is constantly under the pressure caused by modernization, and we have to find novel ways to deal with this pressure. In many countries of this world common humanity is a problem, not a reality and not even an ideal. Powerful movements in the world of Islam preach the jihad against modernity and the jihad is based on the concept of us against them, and so for many Moslims there can be no common humanity. Perhaps we in the West should be less doctrinaire in our claims for human rights, but our discretion will not help us in reaching a common ground with the jihadists, because they do not only want to destroy modernity, but us with it. Our only hope in creating a more peaceful world is that eventually men and women in the world of Islam will want to decide their own fate and will take action against the radicals within Islam.

It is of interest to note what will happen to China in this respect. It seems to be that the mix of an authoritarian regime and economic

---

[17] M. Becker, *The Emergence of Civil Society in the Eighteenth Century. A privileged Moment in the History of England, Scotland and France* (Bloomington 1994: Indiana University Press).

[18] S. Stuurman, *De uitvinding van de Mensheid, Korte Wereldgeschiedenis van het Denken over Gelijkheid en Cultuurverschil* (Amsterdam 2009: Bert Bakker), p. 17.

freedom is a recipe for disaster. The present success of China's economic performance seems to belie this conclusion and perhaps it does. However this success is bought at the cost of enormous pollution. It seems to be the lesson of any authoritarian regime that they are incapable of controlling the excesses of industrial production. Perhaps pollution presents a greater danger to China and the world than an open revolt of Chinese citizens against the state.

The point of this litany of problems is that mankind can only survive by solving them, whether they are problems of violence and war or of pollution. At present there is little hope that we can solve them by peaceful cooperation, and that is the only way we can.

Perhaps the Enlightenment could inspire us to create a new privileged moment. Horkheimer and Adorno were right. We miss the culture to give dignity and elegance to our existence. Their definition of culture, however, will not help us. They refer to culture as the domain of our higher aspirations –a type of cultivation which in German is called *Bildung*– which must function as an antidote against the vulgarity of the world of business in which we spend our daily lives. The effect of this definition of culture is that we escape from the world in which we have to live. Instead, we should try to cultivate the norms of that world of business and no longer regard them as traffic rules we need for negotiating our existence.

Cultivation in this argument takes stock of the values of democracy, justice and freedom. How can we learn the lesson of cultivating them from the philosophers of the Enlightenment? Democracy as we know it, is a nineteenth-century invention. Democracy is necessary on a global scale, I have recently written.[19] Only when every citizen of the world can have a say in the way we create a global community, that attempt can be successful. That lesson we will have to teach ourselves.

Justice and freedom are values cherished in the Enlightenment. How can the essays I have written so far enlighten us? Essay number two on the networking of the Enlightenment can help us to under-

[19] F.L. van Holthoon, "The Necessity of Democratic Regime", *2000. The European Journal*, XII(2), 2011.

Alexander Pope

stand how important it is that –as in the Republic of Letters– we adopt a civilized style of debate as an alternative to the often acrimonious polemics we encounter in the public sphere. Hume was right. Our manners and customs must be able to induce a friendly intercourse and cooperation between individuals. With Lessing (see essay three) we can add to this that a secular morality can go well together with a belief in God. Buffon (essay four) has an important message for us. Man filled the niche in the order of nature and got the task to guide and fashion that order in a responsible manner.[20] The leading theme of Rousseau's writings (essay five) was that man can only be happy leading a simple life. As simple as he thought, life could be we

[20] In her plea for a responsible use of the earth Louise Fresco regards domestication and crop cultivation as an evolution created by man causing new species to exist. L. Fresco, *Hamburgers in het Paradijs, Voedsel in Tijden van Schaarste en Overvloed* (Amsterdam 2012: Bert Bakker), 76.

can not manage it, but it seems true that, if we can escape from the pressure cooker of present change, justice and freedom can prosper in a life with a more leisurely pace. Montesquieu and Hume's analysis of the balance of powers (essay six) remains valuable because it is always important to strike the right balance between authority and freedom. As it is we are inept in having a proper notion of authority, and we do not know to make use of freedom in the public sphere. When we debate the demands of a durable world, it is vitally important that we find the proper balance between authority and freedom. The eighteenth-century economists (essay seven) paid a great deal of attention to a circular flow of goods and regarded a flow without obstruction as a necessary condition for prosperity. If we are thinking in terms of durability, should the theory of a circular flow not deserve a more prominent place in our handbooks on economics? From Sade's life (essay seven) we can learn how dangerous and destructive the sexual drive can be. I discussed him as the black side of the mirror, because the philosophers of the Enlightenment discovered love as a social virtue. Theories of progress in the nineteenth century (essay eight) were not beneficial, and the philosophers did well to have a belief in progress as a manifestation of how mankind could become more civilized without insisting that progress was a necessary outcome. *Les Hommes de Bonne Volonté* could be the motto of the philosophers of the Enlightenment. Ideas are but ideas, but without clear ideas we cannot get on. The philosophers of the Enlightenment can help us to reach them.

I started this series of essays with a motto from Alexander Pope. Let me end this essay and this series with another quotation from Pope:

> That REASON, PASSION, answer one great aim;
> That true SELF-LOVE and SOCIAL are the same;
> That VIRTUE only makes our Bliss below;
> And all our Knowledge is, OURSELVES TO KNOW.[21]

[21] A. Pope, *An Essay on Man. The Poems of Alexander Pope* (London 1965: Methuen), Epistle IV, p. 547, verses 395-398.

A Bibliographical Notice

1. E. Cassirer, *The Philosophy of the Enlightenment* (1932) (Princeton 1979: Princeton University Press).

This book has remained a classical interpretation of the Enlightenment since it appeared in Germany, in 1932. Cassirer was deeply disturbed by the rise to power of the Nazis and his book is a plea for humanity, tolerance and intellectual freedom. Cassirer presents a synthesis of Enlightenment ideas and his attempt is precise and elegant, if somewhat abstract. His least satisfying chapters deal with political ideas and with eigenteenth-century historiography.

The last chapter on aethetics is to the point. Cassirer shows that not only Kant, but also philosophers such as Diderot and Hume accepted aesthetics as being at the basis of all human actions.

2. P. Hazard, *La Crise de la Conscience Européenne, 1680-1715* (Paris 1961 : Fayard), and P. Hazard, *La Pensée Européenne au XVIIIe Siècle, de Montesquieu à Lessing* (Paris 1963 : Fayard).

Hazard wrote two inspiring books on the Enlightenment. Was there a crisis of consciousness at the turn of the seventeenth to the eighteenth century? It certainly was a period of transition, but it seems to me that certain lines of development, which already were in existence, were converging. So, if there was a crisis, it was a crisis caused by this convergence, not because something new occurred. The libertarian scepticism of Montaigne and Gassendi leads to the deism of Toland, Tindal and Bayle. Heterodox currents can be traced in Locke's psychology and Hazard is right in emphasizing the significance of that psychology for the early Enlightenment. The message of Locke's *Reasonableness of* Christianity can be traced back to Grotius. And the propaganda for natural law comes from Grotius, Thomasius, Cumberland. Locke makes use of natural law in a careful and restrained manner. The concept of natural law, however, only had a limited influence on the Enlightenment.

What creates a crisis is Louis XIV's repeal of the Edict of Nantes and the banishment of the Huguenots from France. So the king created a formidable army of protestant critics outside France. For a long time after 1685 the divide between Protestants and Catholics became unbridgeable.

Apart from Locke, two other thinkers played a prominent role in this period. Leibniz in vain tried to bridge the gap between Protestants and Catholics, but his efforts and his philosophy in general emphasized the cultural unity of Europe and that notion certainly promoted the Enlightenment. Pierre Bayle's *Dictionnaire Historique et Critique* was the vademecum for critical spirits, and Locke's *Essay Concerning Human Understanding* made metaphysics an unnecessary exercise, according to the philosophers of the Enlightenment. The period between 1680 and 1715 was the foundation for later developments in the Enlightenment. Hazard indicates this as follows:

> Totale, impérieuse et profonde, elle [the crisis] prépare à son tour, dès avant que le XVIIe siècle soit achevé, à peu près tout le XVIIIe siècle. La grande bataille d'idées a lieu avant 1715, et même avant 1700. Les audaces de l'*Aufklärung*, de l'époque des lumières, apparaissent pâles et menues, à côté des audaces agressives du *Tractatus theologico-politicus*, à côté des audaces vertigineuses de l'Éthique.[22]

Hazard's second book, *La Pensée Européenne,* has the merit of describing the Enlightenment as a European phenomenon, emphasizing its cosmopolitan character. His analysis remains a bit vague and on the surface of things.

3. P. Gay, *The Enlightenment, an Interpretation. The Rise of Modern Paganism* (New York 1968: Vintage); *The Enlightenment, an Interpretation. The Science of Freedom* (London 1970: Wildwood House).

---

[22] P. Hazard, *La Crise*, 418-419.

Peter Gay wrote two surveys of the Enlightenment which give it the most exhaustive treatment so far. His treatment of the German and French Enlightenment is excellent, but that of the Enlightenment in Great Britain is somewhat superficial. Hume is his central figure in that Enlightenment, but in Gay's treatment he becomes an annex of the French Enlightenment, not one of the luminaries on the English and Scottish scene.

As to the whole, I have two critical points to make. They concern the titles of his two books, and as his titles in this case sum up his interpretation, they are important to discuss. In the first volume Gay's argument is that the philosophers of the Enlightenment used classical writers to attack Christianity. That line of attack is unfortunate for two reasons. First, Christian theology and classical philosophy were so much intertwined that the attack on Christianity also involved an attack on Antiquity. When Hume wrote his famous letter to a physician in London he complained that the Classical philosophers were not helpful in solving his spiritual crisis. In a search for new truths, any tradition was an impediment. On the other hand, an attack on tradition did not necessarily mean an attack on Christianity. Gay ignores the many devout members of the Protestant clergy who, at the same time, endorsed the Enlightenment. If we pay attention to the protestant clergy as members of the Enlightenment, we also become aware of the crucial question they were faced with on what to keep of traditions and what to give up.

My second critical point refers to the title of his second volume. *The Science of Freedom* seems to me meaningless and should better be replaced by *The Science of Modernity*. Modernity and secularisation are key-elements of the Enlightenment as I have argued in my text.

Gay does not make the mistake that the philosophers of the Enlightenment, particularly the *philosophes*, were responsible for supplying the ideas of the French Revolution. Gay adds a wondeful paradox to this issue. The American colonists and revolutionaries were the chief beneficiaries of the Enlightenment. They used enlightenment ideas to fashion their own republic.

4. L. Dupré, *The Enlightenment and the Intellectual Foundations of Modern Culture* (New Haven 2004: Yale University Press).

Dupré maintains that the attack on the *Twin Towers* in 2001 was an inducement to write his book. It made him pay special attention to the values of the Enlightenment. He writes:

> The Enlightenment has given us some of our most important ideas: an expressive conception of art, a non-authoritarian view of morality, political theories that build freedom and democracy within the very structures of society.[23]

The quotation portrays the strength and the weakness of his book. What he writes about aesthetics is well done. On the other hand I don't think that his chapter "The Origin of Modern Social Theories" touches the heart of the matter and I have a different opinion of the function of eighteenth-century historiography than the author.

Dupré's treatment of the Enlightenment resembles Cassirer's in the sense that both studies are abstract to a degree. But, as Cassirer's angle is philosophy, Dupré chooses to treat problems on the borderline between theology and philosophy. So his study presents a clear picture of deism. And fortunately he ends his treatment of the Enlightenment on the eve of the French Revolution.

5. J. Israel, *A Revolution of the Mind. Radical Enlightenment and the Origins of Modern Democracy* (Princeton: Princeton 2010); id., *Democratic Enlightenment. Philosophy and Human Rights, 1750-1790* (New York 2011: Oxford University Press).

The first book prints the lectures which Jonathan Israel gave in commemoration of Isaiah Berlin. Israel's central thesis is that the Enlightenment had a radical side and a more conservative one. The radical movement pressed for equality and democracy and Spinoza's philosophy was the source of inspiration for this movement. This thesis raises the following points of criticism:

[23] L. Dupré, *The Enlightenment*, p. 338.

a. Can Spinoza be regarded as the prophet of this type of radicalism? In another context I have expressed my doubts about this.[24] In my estimation Spinoza'd political thinking is rather conventional and if he refers to democracy and the freedom of thought he expresses thought which can be read elsewhere and in a context which is not radical at all. His *Ethica* is indeed a revolutionary work, but the bizarre fact was that it was much discussed, but scarsely read. Spinoza should have had a great influence on the Enlightenment, but he had not. And it is Bayle who is largely responsible for this paradox. People read the lemma on Spinoza in his *Dictionnaire* and people learned that Spinoza was a pantheist and hence an atheist. So they missed the main point of Spinoza's *Ethica.*

b. Can we speak of a radical *movement* in the Enlightenment? This seems not to be the case. The dissenters in England had inherited radical ideas, but in this century they had become orderly citizens. The Quakers are a typical example of this change of behaviour. In the eighteenth century they became well-behaved citizens. The radical opnions of the dissenters returned, when the American Revolution took place. Then writers such as Richard Price and Thomas Paine started to write their radical pamphlets.

It seems wrong to describe the Enlightenment as a split between a radical and a conservative movement. The Enlightenment as a whole was plagued by ambivalences and tensions for which a ready made solution was not in sight. David Miller writes that Hume was a radical epistemologist with a conservative social philosophy. That characterization could be applied to all the philosophers of the Enlightenment. We cannot understand the Enlightenment if we do not accept the fact that these philosophers were quite content with the society of orders in which they lived, or at least accepted it because they saw no alternative to it.

The second book, a hefty tome as Israel prefers to write them, gives a splendid overview of the Enlightenment in its geographical and thematic differentiation. Yet the focus to the Enlightenment is

[24] F.L. van Holthoon, "Spinoza and Hume. Two Different Trajectories", *2000. The European Journal,* 2011, XII(1).

lacking. Sociability is an important aspect of the Enlightenment and networking an important tool of communication. However, Israel is sceptical about the influence of the *salons* (following Lilti?), and according to him the *Encyclopédie* is less important in conveying the ideas of the Enlightenment than is often thought. However it cannot be helped, but the nobility and the bourgeois intellectuals met each other in the *salons* and shaped the conviviality which was so important to the spreading of the ideas of the Enlightenment. It was only a small group which met this way, but the Enlightenment was only relevant to a small group of men.

A discussion of economic ideas is lacking in this volume. And that is a pity. The ideas of the physiocrats in France demonstrate that they were planning far reaching reforms and Hume and Adam Smith across the Channel made clear how economic development could work under the conditions of the emerging capitalism. Religious ideas, according to Israel, can only be regarded as an obstacle to the radical Enlightenment. However, Buisman shows that piety and Enlightenment could easily go together, at least in the Dutch situation.[25]

Of course Israel regards the French Revolution as the logical outcome of the radical Enlightenment. I have given my arguments why I think this view is mistaken. The French Revolution opens a new era and makes that the nineteenth-century interpretation is very different from its eighteenth-century counterpart.

6. *Encyclopedia of the Enlightenment*, (Oxford 2003: Oxford University Press), A.C. Kors chief editor, vol. 1: "Abbade-Enlightenment Studies", vol. 2: "Enthusiasm-Lyceum and Museum ", vol. 3: "Mably-Ruysch", vol. 4: "Sade-Zoology".

These four volumes present a rich variety of subjects, alphabetically arranged. Obviously this is a work meant to be consulted, not to be read through, though it remains wortwhile to read it.

---

[25] J.W. Buisman, *Tussen Vroomheid en Verlichting* (Zwolle 1994: Waanders).

Bibliography of Cited Works

- Adams, J. *A Defence of the Constitutions of Government of the United States* (1797) (Aalen 1979: Scientia Verlag).
- Ariès, Ph., *Centuries of Childhood* (Harmondsworth 1973, Penguin).
- - Aron, R., *Les Étapes de la Pensée Sociologique: Montesquieu, Comte, Marx, Tocqueville, Durkheim, Pareto, Weber* (Paris 1967: Gallimard).
- - Baker, K.M., *Condorcet. From Natural Philosophy to Social Mathematics* (Chicago 1975: University of Chicago Press).
- - Baker, K.M., *Inventing the French Revolution* (Cambridge 1990: Cambridge University Press).
- - Beauvoir, S. de, "Must we Burn Sade?", in Sade, *The 120 Days of Sodom.*
- - Becker, C., *The Heavenly City of the Eighteenth-Century Philosophers* (New Haven 1932: Yale
- - Univesity Press).
- - Becker, M., *The Emergence of Civil Society in the Eighteenth Century. A privileged Moment in the History of England, Scotland and France* (Bloomington 1994: Indiana University Press).
- Ph. Blom, *Wicked Company, Freethinkers and Friendship in Pre-Revolutionary Paris* (London 2011 Weidenfeld & Nicolson).
- - Brown, G., *The Creation of the American Republic, 1776-1787* (New York 1972: Norton).
- - Buffon & Daubenton, *Histoire Naturelle et Générale* (Amsterdam 1766), 1.
- - Buffon, *Les Époques de la Nature* (Paris 1988, Éditions du Museum), J. Roger, édition critique.
- - Buisman, J.W., *Tussen Vroomheid en Verlichting* (Zwolle 1994: Waanders).
- - Burke, E., *Reflections on the Revolution in France* (Gardin City NY: Dolphin).
- - Bury, J. B., *The Idea of Progress* (New York 1955: Dover).

- - Cassirer, E., *The Philosophy of the Enlightenment* (Princeton 1951: Princeton University Press) Koelln F.C.A. & Pettegrove J.P. trans.
- - Chesterfield, Earl of, *The Letters of Philip Dormer Stanhope Earl of Chesterfield* (London 1926: Allen & Unwin) J. Bradshaw ed.
- - Clark, J.C.D., *The Language of Liberty, 1660-1832. Political Discourse and Social Dynamics in the Anglo- American World* (Cambridge 1994: Cambridge University Press).
- - Cobban, A., *Rousseau and the Modern State* (London 1968).
- - Condorcet, *Esquisse d'un Tableau Historique des Progrès de l'Esprit Humain*, 1795 (Paris 1933: Boivin).
- - da Costa, I., *Bezwaren tegen den Geest der Eeuw*, 1823, (Leiden 1923: Sijthoff).
- Craddock, P.B., *Edward Gibbon Luminous Historian, 1772-1794* (Baltimore 1989: Johns Hopkins University Press).
- Darnton, R., *The Literary Underground of the Old Regime* (Cambridge Mass. 1982: Harvard University Press).
- Darnton, R., *The Business of Enlightenment. A Publishing History of the* Encyclopédie, *1775-1800*, (Cambridge Mass. 1979: Harvard University Press).
- - Drouet, J., *Abbé de Saint-Pierre. L'Homme, l'Oeuvre* (Paris 1912: Honoré Champion).
- - Dupré, L., *The Enlightenment and the Intellectual Foundations of Modern Culture* (New Haven 2004: Yale University Press).
- - Emerson, R., *An Enlightened Duke. The Life of Archibald Campbell, Earl of Ilay, 3rd Duke of Argyle*, (Kilkerran 2013: Humming Earth).
- - *The Federalist* (Cleveland 1961: Meridian), J.E. Cooke ed.
- - Foucault, M., *History of Madness* (London 2006: Routledge), J. Khalfos ed. & J. Murphy trans.
- - Fresco, L. *Hamburgers in het Paradijs. Voedsel in Tijden van Schaarste en Overvloed* (Amsterdam 2012: Bert Bakker).
- - Freud, S., *Civilization and its Discontents* (London1961: Hogarth Press).
- - Fukuyama, F., *The End of History and the Last Man* (New York 1992: Free Press).

- - Furet, F., *Penser la Révolution Française* (Paris 1978: Gallimard).
- - Gay, P., *The Enlightenment: An Interpretation. The Rise of Modern Paganism* (New York 1968: Vintage); *The Enlightenment: An Interpretation. The Science of Freedom* (London 1970: Wildwood House).
- - Gibbon, E., *The History of the Decline and Fall of the Roman Empire* (London 1995: Penguin), 3 vols, D. Womersley ed.
- - Gibbon, E., "Vindication", *The History of the Decline and Fall of the Roman Empire* (London 1995: Penguin), D. Wormersley ed., vol. III, app. 3.
- Gibbon, E., *The Autobiography of Edward Gibbon* (London 1923: Dent), D. Smeaton ed.
- Goldberg, R., *Sex and Enlightenment. Women in Richardson and Diderot* (Cambridge 1984: Cambridge University Press).
- Goodman, D., *The Republic of Letters A Cultural History of the French Enlightenment* (Ithaca 1994: Cornell University Press).
- Granpré Molière, J.J., *La Théorie de la Constitution Anglaise chez Montesquieu* (Leiden 1972: Presse Universitaire de Leyde).
- - Grape, C.J., *Les Liaisons Dangereuses de Choderlos de Laclos* (Paris 1997: Gallimard).
- Hazard, P., *La Crise de la Conscience Européenne, 1680-1715* (Paris 1961: Fayard).
- Hazard, P., *La Pensée Européenne au XVIIIe Siècle. De Montesquieu à Lessing* (Paris 1963 : Fayard)
- Helvétius, *De l'Esprit* (Paris 1959: Éditions Sociales), G. Besse ed.
- Hirschmann A.O., *The Passions and the Interest. Political Arguments for Capitalism before its Triumph* (Princeton 1977: Princeton University Press).
- Holthoon, F.L. van, "The Necessity of a Democratic Regime", *2000. The European Journal*, XII (2), Dec. 2011.
- Holthoon, F.L. van, "Sympathy and Utility. A Comparison of the Moral Philosophy of Hume and Smith", *2000. The European Journal*, X(1), 2009.
- Holthoon, F.L. van, *State and Civil Society. Theories, Illusions, Realities. A Survey of Political Theories in the 19th Century Western World* (Maastricht 2003: Shaker).
- Holthoon, F.L. van, *The Road to Utopia. A Study of John Stuart Mill's Social Thought* (Assen 1971: van Gorcum).

- Holthoon, F.L. van, *A Dialogue on David Hume, on his Revision of* a Treatise of Human Nature (Amsterdam 2007: Boom/Amazon.com).
- - Holthoon, F.L. van, "Spinoza and Hume, Two Different Trajectories", *2000.The European Journal*, 2011, XII(1).
- - Holthoon, F.L. van, "The Disappointment of John Adams", *Federalism, Citizenship and Collective Identities in U.S. History*, C.A. van Minnen & S. Hilton eds (Amsterdam 2000: V.U. University Press).
- - Holthoon, F.L. van, *Hume, Leven en Werk* (Kampen 2009: Klement).
- - Holthoon, F.L. van, and Olson D.R., *Common Sense. The Foundations for Social Science* (Lanham MD 1987: University Press of America).
- Holthoon, F.L. van, *Het Gebruik van het Woord Ideologie bij Engels en Marx* (Groningen 1973: Tjeenk Willink) [Inaugural].
- Horkheimer M. & Adorno Th.W., *Dialektik der Auklärung. Philosophische Fragmente* (Frankfurt a. Main 1984: Fischer).
- - Hume, H., *Letters* (Oxford 1969: Clarendon Press).
- - Hume, D., "My Own Life", *Essays Moral, Political and Literary* (Indianapolis 1987: Liberty *Classics*), E.F. Miller ed.
- - Hume, D., *An Enquiry Concerning the Principles of Morals* (Oxford 2006: Clarendon Press), T.L. Beauchamp ed.
- Hume, D., "Of the Origin of Government", *Essays.* Liberty *Classics*), E.F. Miller ed.
- D. Hume, "That Politics May Be Reduced to a Science", *Essays.*
- D. Hume, "Of the Independence of Parliament", *Essays.*
- D. Hume, "Of Refinement in the Arts", *Essays.*
- D. Hume, "Of Public Credit", *Essays.*
- Hume, D., *An Enquiry Concerning Human Understanding* (Oxford 2000: Clarendon Press), T. L. Beauchamp ed.
- - Hume, D., *The History of England* (Indianapolis 1983: Liberty *Classics*).
- Hume, D., *The History of England* (Charlottesville 2000: InteLex), *variorum edition*, F.L.van Holthoon ed.
- Hume, D., *The History of the Reigns of James I and Charles I*, (Harmondsworth: Penguin 1970), D. Forbes, "Introduction".
- Hume, D., *A Treatise of Human Nature* (Oxford 1978: Clarendon Press), P.H.Nidditch ed.

- - Israel, J., *A Revolution of the Mind. Radical Enlightenment and the Origins of Modern Democracy*, (Princeton: Princeton 2010).
- - Israel, J., *Democratic Enlightenment. Philosophy and Human Rights, 1750-1790* (New York 2011: Oxford University Press).
- - Jacob, M.C., *The Radical Enlightenment. Pantheists, Freemasons and Republicans* (London 1981: Allen & Unwin).
- - Kann, R.A., *A History of the Habsburg Empire, 1526-1918* (Berkeley 1977: University of California Press).
- - Kastelein, T., *Groei naar een Industriële Samenleving* (Groningen 1977: Wolters-Noordhoff).
- - Kennedy, E., *A* Philosophe *in the Age of Revolution. Destutt de Tracy and the Origins of "Ideology"* (Philadelphia 1978: The American Philosophical Society).
- - Kinniging, A.A.M, *Aristocracy, Antiquity and History. An Essay on Classicism in Political Thought*, (Leiden 1994: dissertation).
- - Laclos, Choderlos de, *Les Liaisons Dangereuses* (Paris 1995: Garnier), Y. Le Hir ed.
- - Leland, L., *A View of the Principal Deistical Writers* (London 1766: Longman & Dodsley).
- - Lilti, A., *Le Monde des Salons. Sociabilité et Mondainité à Paris au XVIIIe Siècle* (Paris 2005).
- - Lenin, W.J., *The State and Revolution. The Marxist Theory of the State and the Task of the Proletariat in the Revolution, Coll. Works* (Moskou 1974: Progress).
- Lizé, E., *Voltaire, Grimm et la Correspondance Littéraire* (Oxford 1979: The Voltaire Foundation: *Studies on Voltaire and the Eighteenth Century*)
- Lough, J., *The Encyclopédie* (Genève 1989: Slatkine reprints).
- Lovejoy, A.O., *The Great Chain of Being. A Study of the History of an Idea* (New York 1960: Harper).
- Lyons J. & Sloan, Ph.R., *From Natural History to the History of Nature* (Notre Dame 1981 : University of Notre Dame Press).
- Madison, J., *Federalist LI* (ed. Cooke, Meridian books, 351-352).
- Mannheim, K., "Das Konservative Denken", *Wissenssoziologie* (Neuwied 1964: Luchterhand), K.H. Wolff ed.
- Marchal, R., *Fontenelle à l'Aube des Lumières* (Paris 1997: Champion).
- Marcuse, R., *Eros and Civilization. A Philosophical Inquiry into Freud* (New York 1961: Vintage).

- Mauzi, R., *L'Idée de Bonheur dans la Littérature et la Pensée Française au XVIIIe Siècle* (Paris 1960: Colin).
- Meek, R.L., *Social Science and the Ignoble Savage* (Cambridge 1976: Cambridge University Press).
- Meek, R.L., *The Economics of Physiocracy* (London 1963: Allen & Unwin).
- Mill, J.S., *The Principles of Political Economy* (Toronto 1965: University of Toronto Press).
- Mill, J.S., "Whewell on Moral Philosophy" (1852), *Coll. Works*, vol. X.
- Miller, D., *Philosophy and Ideology in Hume's Political Thought* (Oxford 1981: Oxford University Press).
- Millar, J., *The Origin of the Distinction of Ranks* (Bristol 1990: Thoemmes), J.V. Price intr.
- Mittenzwei, I., *Friedrich II von Preussen. Eine Biographie* (Keulen 1980: Pahl-Rugenstein).
- Montesquieu, *De l'Esprit des Lois*, in *Oeuvres Complètes* (L'Intégrale, Paris 1964: Ed. du Seuil).
- Mornet, D., *Les Origines Intellectuelles de la Révolution Française* (Paris 1947: Colin).
- Paine, Th., *The Rights of Man* (Gardin City N.Y.: Dolphin).
- Parsons, T., *The Structure of Social Action* (Glencoe 1949: Free Press).
- Paul, H., *Moeras van de Geschiedenis* (NRCLUX 2012).
- Pinkard, T., *Hegel. A Biography* (Cambridge 2000, Cambridge University Press).
- Pocock, J.G.A, *Barbarism and Religion,* vol. 2, *Narratives of Civil Government* (Cambridge 1999: Cambridge University Press).
- Pocock, J.G.A., *Barbarism and Religion*, vol. 1, *The Enlightenments of Edward Gibbon, 1737-1764* (Cambridge 1999: Cambridge University Press).
- Pocock, J.G.A., *Barbarism and Religion,* vol. 4, *Barbarians, Savages and Empires* (Cambridge 2005: Cambridge University Press).
- Pocock, J.G.A., *Barbarism and Religion*, vol. 5: *Religion: the First Triumph* (Cambridge 2010: Cambridge University Press).
- Pomeau, R., *La Religion de Voltaire* (Paris 1969: Nizet).
- Pomeau, R., *Laclos ou le Paradoxe* (Paris 1995: Garnier).

- - Pope, A., *An Essay on Man.*
- - Popper, K.R., *The Open Society and its Enemies,* vol. 1, *Plato* (London 1962: Routledge & Kegan Paul).
- - Poulain de la Barre, F., *De l'Égalité des Deux Sexes* (1673), (Paris 1984: Fayard).
- - Ricardo, D., *The Principles of Political Economy and Taxation* (London 1965: Everyman's Library).
- - Reinhart, C.M. & Rogoff, K.S., *This Time is Different. Eight Centuries of Folly* (Princeton 2009: Princeton University Press).
- Richardson, S., *Clarissa or the History of a Young Lady*, 1747/1748, (London 1985: Penguin), A. Ross ed. (after the edition of 1798).
- Richardson, S., *Pamela or Virtue Rewarded* (London 1985: Penguin), P. Sabor & N.A. Doody eds.
- - Riesman, D., *The Lonely Crowd. A Study of the Changing American Character* (New Haven 1950: Yale University Press).
- - Rivers, D., *Reason, Grace and Sentiment. A Study of the Language of Religion and Ethics in England 1660-1780*: vol. 1: *Whichcote to Wesley*, vol. 2: *Shaftesbury to Hume* (Cambridge 1991/2001, Cambridge University Press).
- - Robertson Wm., *View of the Progress of Society in Europe*, F. Gilbert ed. (Chicago 1972: University Press of Chicago).
- - Robertson, Wm., *The History of the Reign of the Emperor Charles V* (London 1812: Cadell)
- - J. Roger J., *Buffon. A Life in Natural History* (Ithaca 1997: Cornell University Press), S.L. Bonnefoi trans., L.P. Williams ed.
- - Romein, J., *Aera van Europa. De Eropese Geschiedenis en de Afwijking van het Algemeen Menselijk Patroon* (Leiden 1954: Brill).
- - Trevor Roper H.R., *Religion, the Reformation and Social Change* (London 1977: Macmillan), 19.
- - Rousseau, J.J., *Émile ou l'Éducation, O.C.* (Paris 1969), IV.
- - Rousseau, J.J., *Confessions, O.C.* , I.
- - Rousseau, J.J., *Lettre à C. de Beaumont, O.C.*, IV.
- - Rousseau, J.J., *O.C.* (Paris 1959: Pléiade), I, 1545, note attached to Rousseau's *Confessions.*
- - Rousseau, J.J., *La République de Génève, Discours sur l'Origine et les Fondemens de l'Inégalité*, O.C., III.
- - Rousseau, J.J., *Discours sur l'Économie Politique, O.C*, III.

- - Rousseau, J.J., *Discours sur les Sciences et les Arts, Oeuvres Complètes* (Paris 1964: Pléiade), III.
- - Rousseau, J.J., *Du Contrat Social, O.C.*, III.
- - Rousseau, J.J., *Rousseau Juge de Jean-Jacques, O.C.*, I.
- - Runciman, S., "Gibbon and Byzantium", *Edward Gibbon and the Decline and Fall of the Roman Empire* (Cambridge Mass. 1977: Harvard University Press), G.W. Bowersock ed.
- - Sade, Marquis de, *The One Hundred & Twenty Days of Sodom* (London 1991: Arrow Books), A. Wainhouse & R. Seaver eds.
- - Sade, Marquis de, *Justine. Philosophy in the Bedroom & Other Writings* (New York 1965:Grove Press), R. Seaver & A. Wainhouse eds and transl.
- - Saint-Pierre, Abbé de, *Projet pour la Paix Perpétuelle* (Paris 1986: Fayard).
- - Schumpeter, J.A., *A History of Economic Analysis* (London 1963: Allen & Unwin), E. Boody-Schumpeter ed.
- - Sewell Jr., W.H., *A Rhetoric of Bourgeois Revolution. The Abbé Sieyès and What is the Third Estate?* (Durham 1994: Duke University Press)
- - Shackleton, R., *Montesquieu* (Oxford 1970, Oxford University Press).
- - W. Shakespeare, "Troilus and Cressida", *The Complete Works* (London 1923: Collins).
- - Sher, R., *Church and University in the Scottish Enlightenment. The Moderate Literati of Edinburgh* (Princeton 1985: Princeton University Press).
- - Shorter, E., *The Making of the Modern Family* (Glasgow 1977: Fontana).
- - Skarzynski, W. von, *Adam Smith als Moralphilosoph und Schöpfer der Nationalökonomie* (Berlin 1878).
- - Smith, A., *The Theory of Moral Sentiments* (Oxford 1976: Clarendon Press), D.D. Raphael & A.L Macfie eds.
- Smith, A., *An Inquiry into the Nature and Causes of the Wealth of Nations* (Oxford 1976: Clarendon Press), R.H. Campbell & A.S. Skinner eds, 2vols.
- Smith, A., *Lectures on Jurisprudence* (Oxford 1978: Oxford University Press), R.L. Meek, D.D. Raphael and P.G. Stein eds.

- Spadafora, D., *The Idea of Progress in Eighteenth-Century Britain* (New Haven 1990: Yale University Press).
- Starobinski, J., *Jean-Jacques Rousseau. La Transparence et l'Obstacle* (Paris 1971: Gallimard).
- Stephen, L., *History of English Thought in the Eighteenth Century* (New York 1881: Forgotten Books fac. ed. 2012), 2vols.
- Steuart, J., *An Inquiry into the Principles of Political Economy*, 1767 (Edinburgh 1966: Oliver & Boyd), A.S. Skinner ed.
- Stuart Hughes, H., *Consciousness and Society. The Reorientation of European Social Thought, 1890-1930* (New York 1958: Vintage).
- Stuurman, S., *De uitvinding van de Mensheid. Korte Wereldgeschiedenis van het Denken over Gelijkheid en Cultuurverschil* (Amsterdam 2009: Bert Bakker).
- Talmon, J.L., *The Origins of Totalitarian Democracy* (London 1961: Mercury).
- Thomas, K., *Religion and the Decline of Magic. Studies in Popular Beliefs in Sixteenth and Seventeenth-Century England* (London 1971: Weidenfeld and Nicolson).
- Tocqueville, A. de, *Démocratie en Amérique* (Paris 1990: Vrin), 2 vols.
- - Venturi, F., *Utopia and Reform in the Enlightenment* (Cambridge 1971: Cambridge University Press).
- Vernière, P., *Spinoza et la Pensée Française avant la Révolution* (Paris 1954: P.U.F.).
- Voltaire, *Lettre sur la Tolérance* (1763).
- Voltaire, *Lettres Philosophiques* (Paris 1986: Gallimard).
- Weber, A., *Prinzipien der Geschichts- und Kultursoziologie* (Munich 1951).
- - Williams, D., *Condorcet and Modernity* (Cambridge 2004: Cambridge University Press).
- Winch, D., *Adam Smith's Politics. An Essay in Historiographic Revision* (Cambridge 1978: Cambridge University Press).
- - Womerley, D., *Gibbon and the 'Watchmen of the Holy City. The Historian and his Reputation, 1776-1815* (Oxford 2002: Oxford University Press).
- Zeretsky R. & Scott J.T., *The Philosophers' Quarrel. Rousseau, Hume and the Limits of Human Understanding* (New Haven 2009: Yale University Press).

Index of persons